To my friend
of 58 years who in
my opinion is and has
been the utmost in gymse
hunter - april 30, 1984

Jack Stuart
and
Jo 4/30/84

BIRD DOGS
and Upland Game Birds

Training pointing bird dogs the humane way, specializing in grouse and woodcock dogs.

by Jack Stuart

Edited by
William W. Denlinger and R. Annabel Rathman

Cover design by
Bob Groves

DENLINGER'S PUBLISHERS, LTD.
Box 76, Fairfax, Virginia 22030

Dedication

This book is dedicated to my wife, Ruth, who over the years encouraged and inspired me to attempt this work.

Ruth Stuart.

Library of Congress Cataloging in Publication Data

Stuart, John R.
    Bird dogs and upland game birds.
      1. Bird dogs. 2. Fowling. I. Title.
II. Title: Bird dogs and upland game birds.
SF428.5.S75   1983   636.7'0886   83-14247
ISBN 0-87714-107-X

Copyright © by William W. Denlinger, Fairfax, Virginia 22030.
All rights reserved, including the right to reproduce this book, or portions thereof, in any form, except for the inclusion of brief quotations in a review. This book was manufactured completely in the United States of America.

International Standard Book Number: 0-87714-107-X
Library of Congress Catalog Card Number: 83-14247

Foreword

Dedication to bird dogs is the byword of this book's author. Having been a full-time trainer since 1934, he has learned to understand bird dogs. These years of experience enable him to convey to owners a deeper understanding of their dogs and, in turn, to develop a much closer relationship between dog and owner. Communication is important in all walks of life and especially with bird dogs. A satisfied owner must know *what the dog expects of him*.

Through the years Jack Stuart has developed many innovations to improve the training of class bird dogs. None of his innovations has been punitive in nature; all have been designed to make life easier for both dog and handler.

This publication is both entertaining and informative. Its format is unique in that an experience in the field is related to a training lesson.

In corresponding with Jack over the years, I have appreciated his flair for writing. His devotion to detail and clarity of style should help anyone readily grasp the point being made. Readers will find it difficult to put the book down until they have completed the countless miles of travels with Jack through a learning experience.

Roger C. Fulmer, M.D.

John R. (Jack) Stuart.

Acknowledgements

It pleases me deeply that so many friends have helped in various ways to make this book interesting to owners of pointing bird dogs.

Wally Brzenk came up to our kennel many times to work with the dogs, helping us to illustrate the methods of training for others who are interested in training their own pointing dogs.

John A. (Jack) Nicholson has also given his time to assist me in working dogs so that readers of this work can understand what it takes to train a class gun dog.

I am proud to give credit to my granddaughter, Melaine Allen, an art student at the Minneapolis College of Arts and Design, for her pen and ink sketches. Credit also goes to Kim McGuire and Gail Camstra of Farwell, Michigan, for their sketches. All photos not taken by me are so designated, and appropriate credit given.

There have been friends too numerous to mention who have encouraged me to put my experience in writing so that other pointing dog owners may enjoy and benefit from the short stories as well as the humane method of training that has been successful at Tobacco River Kennels.

I am indeed grateful for the sound advice and help given to me by William F. Brown, editor of The American Field Publishing Company.

The finalizing and arranging of the manuscript was greatly improved with the help of Josephine Stuart.

Preface

It seems to me that what you learn through experience during your lifetime, if worthwhile and valuable, would be wise to pass on to others and not take with you.

I have enjoyed my life's work and would like to share what I have learned about training and hunting through the use of class top-flight bird dogs, especially grouse and woodcock dogs.

While I have hunted grouse and woodcock with various breeds of pointing bird dogs with some degree of success, English Setters have been my prime interest.

The training system described herein is not a cut-and-dried one. It is a leisurely method of training which will produce a well-trained companion gun dog regardless of the pointing breed. Anyone who wants to train and enjoy his own companion bird dog can use this method and be gratified with the success he and his dog will have.

Besides the illustrations, and the training system described throughout this book, the reader will find short stories, which are sometimes a prelude to a training session.

I hope that each story will serve as an interesting lesson in the art of grouse and woodcock hunting, as well as in field hunting with a bird dog.

It might be interesting to readers to know that the author is the inventor of the Stuart Game Bird Releaser, which was the first device of its kind to catapult a live bird into the air in full flight. The Releaser has been available as a training aid since 1949.

The reader will find in these pages various ways of introducing his pointing bird dog to live birds successfully under various conditions.

He will also find that going to his favorite hunting area with a well-mannered companion bird dog and enjoying him with every performance is like a Grand Finale.

I have hunted grouse, woodcock, pheasant, quail, prairie chicken, and Hungarian partridge for over fifty years, and my experiences have been diverse. I have firsthand knowledge of what constitutes a top-flight pointing bird dog, having judged field trials in many areas over the years, as well as having frequently reported grouse trial activities.

It is my aim to keep this book interesting as well as educational.

Table of Contents

A White-and-Black Speckled, Long-Haired Bird Dog 7
Choosing a Bird Dog Puppy, and Kindergarten Training 12
Good Breeding Counts 16
The Way Grouse Dog Puppies are Raised at Tobacco River Kennels 19
The Moocher 22
A Delightful Day on Perry's Creek 23
Tools of the Trade 25
Training Your Dog to Quarter 27
Why Not Hand Signals? 27
How to Yard Train Your Dog 29
Absolute Don'ts 32
Gun-Shy Dogs 32
Helpful Suggestions 33
Don't Expect Too Much From a Puppy 35
Types of Grouse Hunters and Their Dogs 37
Charlie Head's Setter Old Jake and Tobacco River Bill in Alabama 39
What is a Good Pheasant Dog? 40
Spot Hunting 42
Modern-Day Grouse 44
Grouse Tactics 45
Grouse Hugging White Pine Stumps 49
A Welcome Grouse-Hunting Invitation 51
Slab Town 53
Know Something Special About Your Dog 54
You Be the Judge 55
Fred Leggett's Setter Dog Pete 56
What is a Good Grouse Dog? 57
A Dog's First Grouse-Hunting Season 58
What is a Blinker? 59
The Stuart Game Bird Releaser 61
Training Pointing Dogs with the Electronic Game Bird Releaser 64
The Leader 70
The Six-to-Ten-Bird Pigeon Loft 71
Training with Liberated Birds 72
Field Work 77
Jo's Aversion to Woodcock 80
The Shock Collar as a Training Aid 81
The Tattletale Beeper Collar for Cover Dogs 82
The Dog Knows Best 82
How to Make a Dog Release a Firm Grip on a Dead Bird 82
Your Dog's Sign Language 83
Creating a Desire to Retrieve 87
An Amazing English Setter 88
False Pointing 90
The All Day Hunter or Competition Dog 90
"Unproductives" 91
The Finished Pointing Bird Dog 93
The Purpose of Field Trials 97
   Grouse Dog Champions 101
   Field Trial Champions 109
   A Derby Dog 110

WINTER GROUSE by Melaine Allen.

A White-and-Black Speckled, Long-Haired Bird Dog

In the fall of 1918 two men, who have since gone to the happy hunting ground, came up to the ranch near West Branch, Michigan, where I lived at the time with my foster parents, Clarke and Margaret Haire. I will call one man Bob, because I do not remember his name. He had a speckled, long-haired female dog with him called Freckles. I remember the other man well, for he was like one of the family. He was Curtis Gustin—"Curt" for short. Curt often came up during the summer to help out on the ranch. When we had time to spare, he and I would slip off to a trout stream to fish for speckled trout.

This particular day, Curt and his friend with the dog came for a two-day grouse hunt. Grouse were plentiful on the ranch in those days. If you did not find birds every five or ten minutes, you were having a poor day.

I was invited to go along on the hunt because I knew where the good grouse cover was and also knew my way around this thousand-acre ranch. The hunt was to start early on Saturday, the following day.

Clarke Haire called me aside right after the chores on Saturday morning and said, "Curt and Bob are guests, so don't you shoot the birds. Let them do all of the shooting."

I had never hunted with a bird dog; in fact, I had never seen one before that day. As we walked to our first spot to hunt, I asked Curt, "Is that dog a certain breed?"

"It's an English Setter," he replied.

The three of us with that little Setter female started off right after breakfast along the east swamp, hunting toward an old abandoned farm at the edge of our property where there were some old apple trees. Freckles worked out in front and not too wide. As we approached the orchard, she slowed just a little and stopped. Of course, I did not know what she was doing and said to Curt, "The dog is stopped by that sumac near those apple trees." Bob and Curt went up closer and four grouse took wing, one at a time. When the air cleared from those black powder guns, there was not a feather to be found, though the little dog looked all over the area.

We gave up looking for dead birds and went on into the poplar and oak ridges along the far side of the cedar swamp. I learned that when Freckles stopped in a rigid manner it was called pointing.

As we hunted along the ridges, heading in a northerly direction, Freckles pointed six more times in about forty minutes. The men shot every time, but, for some reason, they could not find the target and nary a grouse had been bagged. We then hunted around the low end of the swamp near a marl pit. There were three huge piles of marl stored to be spread later on any soil that appeared to be sour and in need of sweetening. Approaching a thicket between the marl pit and the swamp, Freckles again pointed, and two grouse went out as the men got near, and, again, after the shooting, there were no dead birds. Freckles did not even try to look for a dead bird, and this angered Bob no end. He gave Freckles a good stiff kick in the ribs. I shuddered. She just lay on the ground with a bewildered expression, refusing to even go on hunting as we walked on. After we walked quite a ways, and Freckles did not come, Bob walked back to her, raised his shotgun and said, "I am going to shoot her, she's no /*)@ good!"

At this I said, "If you are going to kill her, why don't you give her to me? I'd like to have her, Bob."

Angrily walking away, he said, "Take her—get her out of my sight, or I will shoot her."

Being only a boy, my hunting clothes were sneakers, blue-bib overalls, a black-sateen shirt, and an overall jacket with pockets full of 12 gauge shells that were loaded with black powder and No. 6 drop shot. I carried an old 12 gauge Peerless single-barrel shotgun that I had found buried in some chaff in the hayloft of an old barn. Having no game pocket or bag, I used a coil of binder twine to tie my dead birds together so that I could carry them over my shoulder.

I walked back to where Freckles still lay on the ground. I sat down beside her, stroking her gently, at the same time talking softly to her. Immediately she crawled into my lap. A feeling of acceptance seemed to come over both Freckles and me. Tying a short piece of binder twine to her collar, I led Freckles north of the barns, where there was an eighty-acre field cleared right in the middle of good grouse cover. Nearing the southeast corner of the field, I bent over and took the binder twine lead off Freckles' collar, and we proceeded about a hundred yards into the woods from the field. The first five minutes or so Freckles walked alongside me when suddenly a grouse flushed some thirty feet ahead, and, as it tried clearing the trees, my old Peerless connected. As soon as that grouse hit the ground, Freckles went and retrieved it to me. For the first time since the kick in the ribs, she wagged her tail. After giving me the bird, Freckles went hunting in earnest and with confidence. When we reached the end of our hunt around the field, which took probably an hour and a half, Freckles had pointed eleven times and we had bagged seven grouse.

Freckles and I went to the house, proudly showing the

birds to Clarke. I also told him what had happened and that Bob had given me Freckles. Clarke said, "You know Bob might change his mind and take Freckles with him when he gets ready to go back to Bay City tomorrow night."

Curt and Bob came in later that evening with one grouse, though they had "walked up" a goodly number of birds and had shot at many.

Saturday night, after feeding Freckles, I fixed a place in the barn for her, and she licked my hand.

Five o'clock in the morning is early, but Sunday was no different from any other day on the ranch. Clarke and I went to the barn to milk the cows and do other chores. Freckles was lying in the manger full of hay where I had left her the night before. She seemed content to sleep a little longer. When the cows were milked and the rest of the chores finished, Clarke said, "Why don't you give Freckles some nice warm milk before we go to breakfast?" That I did.

After breakfast Curt and Bob went to the west side of the ranch where Jackman's Mill used to be. It had long been gone, but some landmarks and old timbers were still visible. This was a good stretch to hunt grouse and woodcock, for it surrounded a huge beaver marsh. Once breakfast was over, I finished some other odd chores before I took Freckles hunting again. We left about ten in the morning, and Freckles and I headed for what was known as the "Big Field." It was three hundred and sixty acres of wild land, all fenced in with good wire fencing. There was a long swamp running up through the middle where all types of evergreens grew; spruce, white cedar, hemlock, balsam, and huge tamarack trees. The swamp ran more or less katty-corner from the southwest corner toward the northeast end of this big field. It also was the lowest place, bordered by tag alders and some gray dogwood. The slopes on either side were not grown up to tall trees as yet, for this was the growth that came on after the harvest of virgin white pine in the late 1800s. The ground cover along here among the sparse aspen, pin cherry, and chokeberry was, for the most part, wintergreen hiding under the bracken. It was the ideal cover for feeding grouse and a nice place to shoot in this sparse tree growth. At the northwest corner was a very high hill. It was covered with white pine stumps, crowfoot grass, and sweetfern. On a bright sunny day this hill was a good spot to go and see far off places, for it was the highest point around. On a clear day, I had once climbed this steep hill and, standing on the highest stump and looking to the east, I had seen Lake Huron, about twenty-five miles away. This hill, with this particular cover, was no place to hunt grouse, but good for sight-seeing.

Freckles quickly went to hunt along the tag alders and soon came to a nice point in the tags where there was a pond-like water hole. When the grouse flushed, it flew right over the pond. As the noise from the shot and black powder smoke cleared away, splashing was heard in the water. Freckles was swimming towards the fluttering bird near the far side of the pond. Taking careful hold of the bird, she swam back across the pond with her prize directly to me. After shaking off the excess water, she went on hunting among the tag alders and dogwood. She came up with four more points; however, only two birds were bagged, for the others had escaped into the safety of the dense swamp. When we came to the end of the swamp, we circled back along the ridge to hunt while we were on our way home, for I was to be back in time for the evening chores. It was about mid-afternoon, and some birds were out feeding in the pin cherries and in the wintergreen on the slopes. Our hunt toward home was a downright pleasure. I couldn't venture to guess how many times Freckles pointed along the ridge.

Freckles and I arrived at the house with eight grouse. Several of Freckles' finds had been from two to four birds, but, with a single-barrel shotgun, one bird on the rise was all that I could get. Nevertheless, we had a good hunt. Because she was only three years old, it looked as if Freckles and I were going to be hunting pals for a long time.

Sunday dinner and supper were all in one, since we would sit down to eat any time from three to four o'clock. Bob and Curt had been so advised. They came in from their hunt just before three.

Clarke had told me beforehand that I should give Bob and Curt the grouse I had. I met them at the back door when they came in for dinner and presented them with the grouse. They grinned as they accepted the birds. I could tell by their expressions that they were very pleased.

After dinner Curt and Bob loaded their gear into Curt's Dodge touring car, enclosed with side curtains. They said goodbye to all of us as they got in the car to head back to Bay City. Bob never looked at Freckles as she stood beside me by the garden gate.

Freckles and I became inseparable as time went on. I fixed her a nice place to sleep right by the house; she was tied up only at night. She went every place with me, even to the "chic sales"—the outhouse in the back yard. Little did I really know about a bird dog back then. Freckles even went after the cows with me, along with our regular cattle dog, a Border Collie called Michael. Freckles never did quite think the idea of working cattle was her dish, as Michael did. She appeared a bit frightened of the cows as they ran at her, and she was very content to walk right alongside me.

One day I went hunting for snowshoe rabbits. Freckles went along, and, after I had shot a couple of snowshoes, she thought it would be nice to chase them, and off she went hunting rabbits. Since she did not bark while chasing them, it was difficult to know where she was. The next time we went rabbit hunting I put a sheep bell on her collar. This worked fine, but, if Freckles came upon a grouse, it took me a few hunts before I realized why the bell stopped ringing so abruptly. You see, her first love was really pointing grouse.

Winter, spring, and summer passed with Freckles going everywhere with me, even when I went after the milk cows on horseback over in Roscommon County, which bordered the ranch on the west side. As fall followed the summer and the frosts came, Freckles and I became itchy to get into the woods and hunt for the new crop of grouse. We went every chance we got. Going to a country school two miles away and doing the chores left little time. There were no school buses in those days. We went on "shanks' mare." Between chores on Saturday and Sunday, Freckles and I would get in some good licks at grouse hunting.

Under the eaves of the back of the house, I had strung a piece of stovepipe wire where I would hang the grouse by their heads when we came in from hunting. At night the temperature dropped to freezing and the grouse kept well. When I would shoot a grouse, I would remove and examine the crop so that I could learn what the birds were feeding on. That way, I knew where to hunt. Also the "innards" would be removed, thus making the birds keep longer when hanging under the eaves. The eaves on the north side of a house or a cabin are the best for preserving game, because of the colder temperatures.

I learned to remove the crop and innards from the grouse from a neighbor, Mrs. Ferguson, who taught me how to hunt and shoot grouse on the wing when I was twelve years old. Mrs. Ferguson was an excellent wing shot. She, too, shot a single barrel—a 16 gauge shotgun. She would carry an extra shell in her left hand directly under the barrel of the gun. Many times I saw her shoot a grouse, immediately reload, and hit a second bird when there might be three or four birds getting out from under an old apple tree or thornapple shrub. Thus I learned wing shooting grouse from Mrs. Ferguson.

It was past the middle of October when word came from Curt Gustin that he and Bob would be up that Friday night to hunt grouse on Saturday and Sunday. They arrived late Friday night in Curt's Dodge. Freckles followed me out in front of the house when I went out to greet them, and, as soon as she heard Bob's voice, she went right back to her doghouse.

Since Margaret always had coffee and some goodies baked, we had a snack and went off to bed to be rested for the grouse hunting the next day.

Clarke and I were up at five o'clock, as usual, for the early morning routine with the milk cows. This time Clarke told me that I could shoot at the grouse since the dog worked so well with me.

After breakfast we headed toward some of the fields on the south side of the ranch, for all of them were surrounded by excellent grouse cover. The Beaver Meadow Creek, a trout stream, meandered on the low side and around three or four of these fields. Much of the woods were small patches, but since it was quite a distance across the fields to the next woods, the grouse would fly back and forth in the same patch of woods when flushed.

We first hunted the alders along Beaver Meadow Creek and Freckles worked the alders well, pointing many times. The birds were a bit flighty early that morning since it was slightly windy. That is why we hunted the heavy cover along the creek. If the birds flew straight through the alders, it was nearly always a clean miss. The shooting was more productive when a grouse went more or less straight up to clear the alders.

After Freckles had pointed several grouse and retrieved three birds, Bob said to Curt, "It looks as if Freckles has gotten over her shyness." I had never found her to be shy, but I did notice that she would not hunt in front of Bob if she could find a way to keep from doing it.

We crossed an old fence, heading for a small woods at the far side of what had been a corn field that summer. The shocked corn was still in the field. The woods produced four finds for Freckles. Curt and Bob both agreed that I was to shoot whenever I could get a decent shot, since they wanted to take back a nice bag of birds to show their friends in Bay City. I was happy to do this, because I loved watching Freckles point and retrieve a bird. It was sheer joy. In the four finds there must have been seven or eight grouse, but only three were killed. Freckles was again doing her duty as a bird dog.

We left this patch of woods, going across the south side of the ranch to Bill Smart's place. Bill Smart was an elderly, gray-haired man with a whimsical smile. He had lots of wild land. Bill lived in a cabin-like shack by himself, more or less as a recluse. He had one horse, a milk cow, and a few chickens. He was a witty but lonesome man and always seemed exceedingly happy when I would stop by for a visit whenever I was anywhere near his place. Few people ever stopped to visit "Old Bill," as he was called by some of the neighbors. I got the feeling from the way some of them talked about "Old Bill" that they thought he was a bit odd, or "tetched," but what did a twelve-year-old boy know about that as long as the old man was nice to him, an orphan boy? Bill would always say, as I was leaving his place, "You come back and visit with me soon, and you can hunt on my place anytime."

The three of us and Freckles went through the gap into Bill Smart's woods. We had barely gotten into the woods when Freckles pointed right off the old trail that led to Bill's shack. The side hill she was pointing into was covered with pin cherry trees, and some sweet clover grew under the trees. When I stepped alongside Freckles, there was an eruption of grouse from the dense sweet clover under the cherry trees. There must have been eight or ten grouse in that covey. When the smoke cleared away, Freckles could be seen hunting dead birds. She made short work of retrieving three grouse to me.

Since the three of us had bagged eleven grouse, we decided to go back to the house, which was about a mile and a half across the fields. Walking along the little roads near the ends of the fields made the trek back to the house quicker and easier.

It was very noticeable while we walked along that Freckles did not want to be near Bob. If he walked near me, she would go around on the far side of me, staying close to my side. She only tolerated him while hunting, and I noticed a couple of times, when he got quite close to her while she was on point, that she would stand and tremble, but never leave her bird or run in and flush it.

As we walked along, Curt said to Bob, "That farm boy Jack sure can shoot grouse. If we didn't have him along, we wouldn't get enough grouse to stink up a frying pan." I think I swelled with pride a little at that remark from Curt.

Bob said, "Curt, let's just hunt a couple hours in the morning tomorrow because I have to be back in Bay City for a meeting at five o'clock.

"That's fine with me," Curt replied. He then turned to me and asked, "Can you go with us right after the chores?"

"I'll ask Clarke when we get home," I answered.

Curt helped with the chores Saturday evening and told Clarke that he would help again in the morning. This made it easy for me to get permission to go hunting with Curt and Bob again on Sunday morning.

When Margaret learned that the men were going to leave for Bay City shortly after noon on Sunday, she planned an early dinner of chicken and biscuits with her golden-yellow chicken gravy. Margaret was famous for a special treat—popovers filled with fresh, farm-whipped cream.

On Sunday Curt helped me with the chores before breakfast and we ate early. As we were leaving to hunt, shortly after eight o'clock, Margaret called to us, "You bird hunters be in before twelve because the dinner will be ready right at noon."

Curt asked me where I thought we should go to find some grouse that would not be too far from the house. I suggested that we hunt west along the old Hoffman Branch grade as far as Jackman's Mill, then south toward the Hickey ranch along Norm's Creek, another stream where Curt and I had spent many hours brook-trout fishing the previous summer.

While we hunted our way along the Hoffman grade, Freckles spent most of her time on the left side, since there was a wire fence on our right for about a half-mile. The shooting there was mostly in tag alders, but we managed to pick up two grouse that Freckles pointed before we got to Jackman's Mill, where we turned south on a siding grade toward Norm's Creek. The rails and ties had been removed from the grade shortly after the timber had been logged off. They were nice places to hunt, because every once in a while, a grouse in the thicket on the side would flush near the edge of the grade and fly right down the grade ahead of us, becoming an easy open target.

Reaching Norm's Creek, we hunted down the south side of the creek for about an hour, and, again, Freckles proved she knew this grouse-hunting business by having six good finds. But the shooting wasn't all that easy here, and we managed to bag only two grouse. We discovered that we were on the better side of the creek when we crossed over it on an old log, as we worked our way back towards the Hickey ranch grade. We picked up two more grouse that Freckles found.

"When we get back to Jackman's Mill, let's hunt our way home. It's a little after ten o'clock. Besides, we have birds enough," said Curt.

"We have plenty of time to get our limit. Why quit early?" Bob queried.

Curt replied, "Jack is giving us all the birds, and we don't need to get more. You can have your limit of what we have, and I'll take what is left."

Since Freckles had hunted hard for two days now, she hunted close on either side of the Hoffman Branch grade. She worked ahead on our left. As we were nearing the end of the cover, she came out and stood staunchly right on the grade.

"Curt, you go up there and get that bird for Freckles," I said.

He went right up alongside the dog. The grouse flushed high into the trees. When Curt's shot connected, the grouse toppled into heavy cover. Freckles retrieved the bird right to Curt. He turned to us and said, "By George, I know I got that grouse without any help."

The house could be seen from where this last grouse was taken, and, as we neared the house, the aroma of Margaret's chicken and biscuits was evident. Our steps quickened somewhat, for we were all hungry. Even Freckles raised her nose into the air towards the house. I was sure she figured on some of that good gravy on her food, too.

Curt and Bob went up to the screened front porch where Clarke was waiting to let them in. I took Freckles around to the back of the house and snapped her chain on her by her doghouse, where I sat by her with my arm around her neck, thinking what a nice dog and companion I had. Margaret called that dinner was on and for everybody to get washed up.

Clarke and Margaret both had learned to like Freckles, too. Even Michael, the stock dog, got along well with her, though most of the time he was allowed to sleep in the back room of the house, which was also the place we stored the firewood for the kitchen range.

Clarke and Margaret were people who believed in talking things over during a meal. The conversation of the grownups was active as we all enjoyed the dinner, complete with homemade goodies such as freshly baked bread. In fact, everything on the table except the sugar, salt, and pepper, was produced right there on the ranch.

As everyone neared the end of this main Sunday dinner, Margaret left the table and returned from the kitchen with a huge plate of her delicious popovers filled with whipped cream. It was rather difficult for us to push ourselves away from the table when we were finished.

Bob said, "Curt, I'll load the guns and duffle in the car while you get the rest of the birds from back of the house."

I helped Curt with the birds and walked to the car with him to bid them goodbye. Curt got in behind the steering wheel, but Bob stood by the car, and turning to Curt said, "I'll get my dog."

Clarke heard him say that. I stood in the road almost stiff. I just couldn't believe what I'd heard until I saw Bob come dragging Freckles by the collar, since she was very reluctant to go with him. As Bob put Freckles in the back seat of the car, I ran as fast as I could to the back of the house, crying every step of the way. Sitting down on the pump base, near Freckles' doghouse and where her chain lay on the ground, my crying spell turned into a heaving sort of sob so profound that I thought my chest would burst.

Clarke came and sat down with me, trying to console me, telling me, "You know the dog was really his."

Between sobs I kept saying over and over, "No, no, he was going to shoot Freckles, and he gave her to me." Blurting between trying to cry and sobbing, I said to Clarke, "When I grow up, I'm going to get me one of those white-and-black speckled, long-haired bird dogs just like Freckles."

Clarke, patting me on the shoulder, said, "That's my boy, Jack. You will, I'm sure.

To help me forget, that Sunday evening Clarke did some of the little chores I usually did. Sleeping, for me, came very hard that night, for I still could not believe what had happened. It was a long time before I got Freckles off my mind.

Curt called the ranch one night late in October 1920, saying that he was coming up to go grouse hunting with me. I shuddered a little at first when Clarke told me Curt was coming.

Curt drove in on a Friday night just after dark. He was alone. We all visited until it was time for bed.

Curt arose early the next morning and helped with the chores so that he and I could go bird hunting after breakfast. Curt was too nice a person to open up an old wound, and there was never a word exchanged about Freckles while we walked up our grouse and hunted for our dead birds. Curt's actions indicated that the hunt was not the same as the one two years before, and, before leaving for Bay City, he said, "I have never fished or hunted with Bob again since that Sunday we left the ranch with your dog. I didn't say four words to him all the way back to Bay City."

I never saw Freckles again. Of all the dogs that I have had and worked with the last fifty years, none has ever been called Freckles. One that I "worked" for Andy Eaton of Beaverton, Michigan, was named Freckles, but I would not call him by that name. As far as I was concerned, he was always called Buddy.

While there are plenty of good breeds of bird dogs, it is plain to see why I chose English Setters. There will never be another Freckles.

Freckles looked like this English Setter.

Choosing a Bird Dog Puppy, and Kindergarten Training

Regardless of what breed of pointing dog you choose to buy, try to acquire a puppy from a place where you have hunted with its parents, so you are satisfied the dog is from good hunting stock. This does not always mean that you are going to get a topnotch puppy, but percentage-wise, your chances of developing a good hunting dog are much better. If this cannot be done, go to a reputable kennel where the operator has a good, systematic breeding program and a reputation of producing topnotch shooting dogs.

Speaking of breeds to choose from, there are many, and the choice is yours to make. If you have never owned or hunted birds with a pointing bird dog, a good choice would be a Pointer, English Setter, Brittany, German Shorthaired Pointer, or Viszla. The last three breeds are not generally so popular as the English Setter or Pointer. If you are primarily a grouse hunter, the Setter would probably be a good choice, for this breed hunts the briars more easily and better than the Pointer. Also, the Setter withstands the cold weather better because of its heavier coat. Besides the English Setter, there are two other Setter breeds that are growing in popularity as grouse dogs: namely, the Irish (red) Setter and the all black-and-tan Gordon Setter. The Gordon Setter usually works closer than the other breeds. I have worked all of the above breeds, plus a number of other pointing breeds, during the last fifty years, but the ones I have mentioned in the order written are the best choices, in my opinion. However, your selection of a particular breed is strictly a matter of individual preference.

It is wise when looking for a puppy, from whomever you choose to buy, to go into the background, breeding, pedigree, and so forth. Many times one will have a bitch that does not come up to standards in one or more respects. You will hear it said, even though the bitch is mediocre, or not even a really good bird dog in the field, "She will make a good brood bitch." This is not always true. And no matter how good the stud dog might be, he cannot claim all the honors in producing a good litter. In fact, many times through the years I have talked to well-known trainers who also breed and sell bird dogs, and the information I gathered from just about all of them was that the bitch, through her influences during their first six weeks of life, contributes from sixty-five to eighty percent towards the know-how and capabilities of her offspring. This has also been the case in my breeding program. If this is true generally, then the better the bitch, the better the puppies.

When choosing a puppy, try to look at a litter that is from ten to twelve weeks of age, instead of five or six. If you see the whole litter running around in a good-sized area where they are free to show themselves off in a natural manner, watch for the one that ignores the rest of his litter mates and goes looking for anything that flies, be it butterflies, grasshoppers, or whatever. If you want to have a dog that is classy when it matures, take note of how high up on the buttocks the base of the tail is set; also, how happy and how high the tail is when the puppies are moving about. Now look for a good, deep-chested individual with the front legs not close together. His hind legs should move out rather squarely and wide apart when he runs, with hocks straight up and down. If he runs or stands with his hocks in toward each other, he will tire easily and, most likely, will not have a desirable gait when he grows up.

Now that you have chosen your puppy, be sure to find out when he was treated for parasites (roundworms and hookworms). Also, check to see if he has been vaccinated for canine distemper, parainfluenza, hepatitis, leptospirosis, and Parvo-Virus. A one-shot, four- or five-way vaccine can be given three or four weeks after the puppies have been weaned. Don't take chances—have your puppy vaccinated just as soon as you acquire him.

As to when to start training, it is said that a dog's age, in comparison to man, is seven-to-one; for example, a dog one year old is comparable to a boy seven years old, or if you wish to think of age by the month, a nine-month-old puppy is comparable to a five-year-and-three-month-old boy going to kindergarten. Without a doubt, this boy has had some preschool training, which can be done right at home by parents, brothers, and sisters in daily activities, and we think little about it—we just take it for granted.

You acquire a puppy twelve weeks old; why not provide preschool training? Name your puppy and always call him by name. You can easily teach him to come by using the word "come" at feeding time. Turn him loose in his play yard, show him the feed dish, but let him run around. When he is looking in your direction, set the feed dish down and, at the same time, if his name is Pete, say, "Pete, come." You will be surprised at how quickly he associates the command with you and the food. I mentioned earlier that you should name the puppy when you acquire him. Always give him a one-syllable name, such as Joe, Pete, or Bill. A name like this is easier for the dog to hear.

Puppies working on a grouse wing on a fishing pole.

Now that the preliminaries have been taken care of and you are the proud owner of a well-bred puppy with the conformation that you wanted, and your plans are to have a good shooting dog and companion, you can continue with simple training such as "sit," and you can even start teaching "whoa" when you feed him. Do not do this by whacking him with your hand or a newspaper; rather, hold him a few feet away from his feed pan and stroke him lightly; at the same time softly say "whoa" several times, then lightly tap him on the head twice—tap, tap. This means he can eat. Do this every time you feed him for two weeks, and you will be surprised at how smart he is. Don't be afraid to show affection for your puppy. Don't cuss at him; talk softly to him and he will, as he learns and grows, become the hunting companion you have been looking for. You can do this preschool training in the dog's play yard.

Pups can begin looking for live birds when they are four months old, starting with common barn pigeons, and a little later, bob-white quail. Complete details of how this is done is described in the chapter "Training Pointing Dogs with the Electronic Game Bird Releaser."

Feeding is very important. A three-month-old puppy should be fed three times a day—morning, noon, and night—until he is six months of age, and twice a day—morning and evening—until he is a year old. Nearly all of the major dog food companies now make special puppy foods, which are very good and should be fed to the puppy until he is one year old. He then can go on to a top name brand of regular dog ration. If your dog lives in the house, or is allowed in at night, I suggest feeding him each morning rather than in the evening. He is less apt to be uncomfortable and have an accident in the house during the night. Here is another bit of advice: if you purchase a very young (five- or six-weeks-old) puppy and keep him in the house, he is likely to cry and carry on at night until he forgets about his mother. Wrap up an alarm clock and put it in his box with him. The ticking of the clock will lull him to sleep and take his mind off his problem.

Now that you have properly cared for your young dog, he is ready for advanced yard training. What you have done so far is only preschool. Now I am going to "try to get in good with the ladies." By this I mean that you, the one who is going to train and hunt with the dog, should feed him and care for him if you possibly can. The dog will know you and respond more readily if you give him personal care and attention. Your future gun dog should now be taught yard work in earnest.

Attach a check cord about thirty feet long to his collar and have him sit. Teaching him to sit is quite simple. Have the dog stand facing you. Hold the cord in your left hand, reach over and take hold of the dog's back just ahead of his hips, and say "sit." At the same time squeeze and push down on his back. As soon as he sits, release the pressure with your right hand. This may have to be repeated several times.

Fastrain, by Champion Jetrain ex Moxie Crockett, pointing a butterfly in his play yard at eight weeks of age.

When one of the littermates points, the others should honor or back—no matter how they look doing it.

I like to use the word "whoa," rather than confuse the dog with "sit" and "stay." Why? Any time the dog is given a command where he is not to move, "whoa" is the word. It will pay off well later on.

Now that he is sitting on command, hold on to your check cord and slowly walk around the dog. Make the circle around him small at first so that, if he gets up or moves, you can put him back in the sit position and start over. Soon you can make the circle bigger with good results. Once straight in front of the sitting dog, squat down or kneel on one knee and give the command "come." If he just sits, give a tug on the check cord and follow it immediately with the word "come." Most dogs learn the command quickly.

Start walking around with the dog, still having control with the check cord. Now and then stop and say "sit." Do not walk straight away in front of the dog. Give the command "whoa" and take one step to the side of the dog. If he remains, take another step to the side, and if he still remains, walk straight out and across so that you are directly in front of the dog, and then go through the "come" routine as you did earlier. The "come" procedure can also be worked using a whistle in conjunction with the word "come"; however, if you wish to use a whistle, blow it in a low rolling tone followed immediately by the word "come." It is important that you use the whistle in this manner so that the dog associates the rolling tone with the order to "come," because later on you will use the whistle in a different way for a different reason.

The above yard-training lessons should be taught first. If you're teaching one lesson such as "sit," each day when you work the dog, start with the "sit" lesson before going to the next lesson. It will be more impressive to the dog, and the results will be better. I am one who believes in teaching a young dog all he can learn while he is still young enough to be controlled, and that's very important if you want to have a good gun dog when he reaches the end of his training—if there is such a thing as an end to his training. For this reason, it is important to get your dog into birds before he is six months or older—up to one year—before he develops bad habits such as chasing deer or rabbits. The dog can be broken from both of these bad habits. Why do it the hard way? Birds will be the dog's first love if he is exposed to them often enough and while he is young enough. There are ways this can be done even in the off-season or in the summer. At the same time that you are introducing your young dog to birds, you can also employ the yard training he has already acquired so that he will start putting it all together.

Normally I do not teach a dog to heel until his second year, or Derby age. Also, at Derby age, I insist on the term "whoa" even more emphatically than at the earlier age.

Up to now nothing has been mentioned about introducing your young dog to the gun. I do not use the gun to call the dog to his feed; rather, it has proved better to first introduce the gun, loaded with a .22 blank cartridge, when he also is getting acquainted with live birds. Initially, whether he points or not, as long as you are sure that he has contact with a bird and that he is in the process of chasing the bird, let him chase some distance before you shoot. He will associate the sound of the gun with the bird. You can, when you are convinced he is enjoying this experience, shoot while he is closer to you and while the bird is still within killing distance while flying. If you follow this procedure, you will not have a gun-shy dog. Gun shyness is usually a man-made characteristic. (See the chapter "Gun-Shy Dogs.")

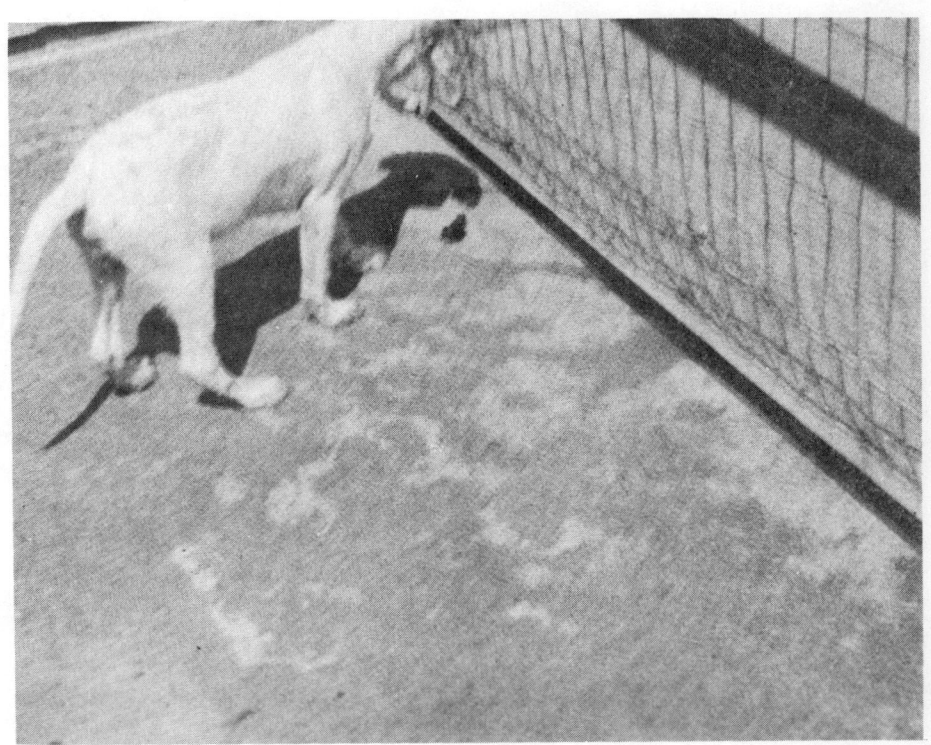
Fastrain, pointing a toad in his kennel run. This is called toad style.

Fastrain, pointing a grouse wing at nine weeks.

Good Breeding Counts

In the winter of 1972, my wife and I took our string of dogs to Crossville, Tennessee, for training on and around the Cumberland Plateau, where the bird population consisted of quail, ruffed grouse, and woodcock. Our dogs were comfortably chained to their new kennels, which were telephone cable spools set on end on cement blocks, with an entrance hole cut in the center hub of the spool and an eye bolt fastened to the flange on the bottom of the spool, where each dog was chained so it easily could go into its bed of fine hay.

A conservation officer called to say that he would take me around to some places to hunt quail and show me areas where I could hunt grouse. We hunted together several days. The officer had a white-and-black Pointer female about four years old. However, she seemed to have trouble handling a covey of quail, mostly because every time she looked as if she was about to point, her owner would scream and run at her and then trounce her good because the covey flushed.

I had worked three different dogs with this man and his Pointer over a period of five days. Each of my three dogs would back a pointing dog well and made every effort to back this Pointer the first three days. On the fourth day they ignored the Pointer and ran around in front and three different times stole the point. Being concerned about this, I quit hunting my dogs with this Pointer.

A week or so later, I came in one evening from working the dogs to find a man at our cottage visiting with my wife. He has a wonderful personality and is a gentleman of the first water. With a formal introduction, I learned that his name is George Hudson. If there is anyone more "doggy" than I am, it has to be George. He has first-class knowledge of good breeding, especially of English Setters, and is an ardent hunter of grouse, woodcock, and quail. He knows how a good bird dog should do its job.

I soon learned that George was a "walking encyclopedia" when it came to Setter breeding, which brings me up to one day when George and I went to a wooded area at the very edge of the city limits of Crossville. It looked more like a grouse woods than quail cover, but George assured me that there could be quail here, too. Since my Setter, Tobacco River Doctor, had been giving me trouble about backing after working several times with the white-and-black Pointer previously mentioned, I asked George if I could work Doc with his two-year-old Setter female, Jordan's Peerless Meg, called Maggie. I told George I would drag a check cord on my belt so that when Maggie pointed, I could bring Doc in to back. After the two dogs had hunted only a few minutes, Maggie pointed stylishly directly in front of us. Doc was coming in from the right some distance away and backed nicely without any help from me. George flushed a woodcock in front of Maggie and shot it. Maggie quickly went to retrieve. I noticed that, when she was about halfway to where the woodcock dropped, she hesitated for an instant but went on, picked up the woodcock, and started returning with it. When she reached the place where she had hesitated, she pointed high and intensely with the woodcock in her mouth. George walked thirty feet in front of Maggie and flushed a large covey of quail.

Maggie had Crockett bloodlines on the top line (her sire's side) and had well-known dogs such as Turnto, Mississippi Zev, Commander's Hightone Beau, and many Peerless Setters on the bottom line (the dam's side) of her pedigree. So good breeding does count towards producing good offspring.

My wife, Ruth, and I spent many hours with George, his lovely wife, Melba, and their two children, Brett and Leigh, during the winter of 1972 and again during the winter of 1979. Incidentally, Melba is famous for her Southern "banana puddin'."

When the time came for us to return to our Tobacco River Kennels in Michigan, we leased Jordan's Peerless Meg from George. We bred her to Tobacco River Pirate, and the Tobacco River Kennels then branched out into the Crockett line of Setters with which we are very satisfied. In our kennel at this time are Tobacco River Crockett, Crockett Maggie, Moxie Crockett, and Bodacious. Bodacious is a full brother to Tobacco River Crockett but not a litter mate; he is five years younger.

Fastrain, five months old, pointing a single quail during a short workout.

Fastrain, pointing a covey of quail in the pine woods near Jack, Alabama, at eleven months old.

Tobacco River Pirate pointing quail in Alabama, his daughter Crockett Maggie honoring him.

A long view of the kennel runs, from the south end. Tobacco River Crockett is in the first run.

Jack Stuart, looking at one of his Setters at Tobacco River Kennels. At the far end of the gutter there are two four-inch drain escapes; one is for surface water and the other leads to a septic tank. Photo by Wally Brzenk.

The Way Grouse Dog Puppies are Raised at Tobacco River Kennels

At Tobacco River Kennels there are two fenced-in yards each forty feet square. In the center of each is a roomy doghouse with a lift top for easy access when caring for the bitch and her puppies. The bitch is transferred from the main kennel to this puppy yard three weeks before the puppies are due in order to become acclimated to her new environment.

Proper food for the bitch is essential, as is an ample supply of fresh water. When the puppies arrive, the bitch is fed twice daily her regular ration mixed with warm cows' milk instead of water.

The doghouse is fixed on cement blocks. On either side of the doghouse is a four- by six-foot lean-to made of three-quarter inch all weather plywood. These lean-tos provide shade for the bitch and the puppies. On the outer side of the lean-to, lath-type cleats, two feet long, are nailed about four inches apart from the ground edge to the top, which is near the roof of the doghouse. When the puppies are almost ready to be weaned, they will already be playing among themselves. In a few days they will try to climb up the cleats on the lean-to. Only a few days later, they all will be running up one lean-to and down the other. This develops good strong legs and chests on the puppies naturally.

Empty Pet Milk cans are loaded with a couple of ounces of bird shot, then the holes are soldered tightly. With the cans in the puppy yard, the pups can roll them around, get accustomed to the noise, and have fun at the same time. A small-sized nylon cord twelve to fifteen feet long has a dog bell tied into it every three or four feet. This is fastened across the top of the puppy yard fence near one corner. Three or four drop cords are fastened a couple of feet apart to the cord with the bells and are allowed to hang nearly to the ground. The puppies soon learn to grab the drop cords, ringing the bells vigorously.

Once the puppies are weaned and on commercial food, they should have access to clean, dry puppy foods and fresh water at all times. If it is desired to feed puppy food moistened, the puppies should be fed small amounts four times a day until they are twelve weeks old; then three times a day until six months of age; and twice a day, night and morning, until one year old. Most top-quality dog food companies make a special puppy food with all the nutrients puppies need to develop fully.

Puppies reared in the above manner will be strong, and never shy. An important after-weaning treatment for the bitch: as soon as she is taken away from her puppies, turn her on her side and thoroughly rub her "faucets" with camphorated oil. This should be done three or four times a day the first week, then twice a day until the milk dries up.

Our Crockett Maggie bitch has had forty-nine puppies, is now nine years old, has been treated with camphorated oil after each litter, and does not have one faucet any larger than an eraser on a lead pencil. Maggie says, "I am proud; I am not underslung."

After the puppies are weaned and are from six to eight weeks old, it is time to find out if they will use their noses to advantage. The following is a proven way to find out: Use small bits of sharp cheese to test the litter of puppies; allow them to smell it and eat it. It is a special treat for them, and it's a joy to watch them get so excited over this new discovery. A couple of days later, small pieces of the same kind of sharp cheese are hidden in the higher grass along the fence in the big yard. The puppies are all let out to play in the yard. In most litters there is one puppy who finds the cheese more quickly than the others. That puppy usually remains in the Tobacco River Kennels for further development. He always proves to have a keen nose for bird hunting also. Try it.

Crockett Maggie says, "My forty-nine puppies are all over the United States and Canada."

Fascia's Nick ex Moxie Crockett litter, four weeks old, at the feed pan. Moxie Crockett is in the background.

I'm not stuck—just checking on my brothers and sisters.

Four is a crowd. Look at the legs and chests on these ten-week-old Setter puppies.

Tuckered out.

The Moocher

While this has nothing to do with actual grouse hunting, it does have a bearing on a ten-day grouse-hunting trip that Lloyd Carlisle, Alex Adams, and I, all from Port Huron, Michigan, went on to Cedar Lake, near Oscoda, Michigan, in the fall of 1937.

We arrived at the cottage on the lake in the late afternoon, took care of our bird dogs, had a bite to eat, then decided we would go to Oscoda and phone our wives to let them know that we had arrived at our camp safely. In town we came upon an old-fashioned drugstore--a large, roomy, high-ceilinged store, with the old-fashioned wire-back chairs and ice cream tables to match.

A tall, pleasantly neat man was the owner. He gladly gave us permission to use his wall phone in the far corner. Since Lloyd decided to call his wife first, Alex and I sat in a couple of chairs that were nearby. I had no more than gotten seated when a beautiful white-and-black-ticked Setter dog walked up to me, holding a paper plate in his mouth. He stood there looking at me with his big brown eyes and wagged his tail. I asked the owner, "What is the purpose of the dog's action?"

"He wants you to put a nickel on the plate so that he can get some ice cream," he replied.

I did. The dog carried the plate to the owner, who in turn took the nickel after placing a scoop of ice cream on the plate. The Setter then carried the plate of ice cream to the back room and ate it. However, he was back in a couple of minutes mooching another nickel for more ice cream.

Before we three had all completed our calls to our wives, that Setter had begged seventy-five cents from us and had eaten fifteen scoops of ice cream. Sure, he was fat.

A good head study of an English Setter.

A Delightful Day on Perry's Creek

One day in 1935, I decided to go up to Ogemaw County and fish for brook trout on Perry's Creek, where I had fished as a boy with a wild cherry fishing pole and a Prince Albert tobacco can full of fish worms. I would have a half-dozen hooks that I had begged off our neighbor, Charlie Post. With a piece of ordinary bag string for a fishing line and a small washer for a sinker, one of Charlie's hooks loaded with a nice fat garden hackle, and, to carry home my catch, a sugar sack tied at the top corners with a piece of binder twine, I would be ready to invade Perry's Creek.

Of course, things had changed considerably since I was a boy. Everything appeared to be half as big; that is, all except the stream itself. That seemed to have remained much the same as when I was a boy.

I parked my car some distance from where I wanted to start fishing. I approached the big tube that served as passage for the stream going under the dirt road. Many memories popped into my mind as I stood on the road over that large tube that had once been a retort furnace at the turpentine plant west of Perry's Creek, up the old Hoffman Branch railroad grade (now a two-track wagon trail), all the way to Clear Lake, where the turpentine plant was located years ago. The turpentine plant workers went each day to what was called "The Plains" in those days, with a team and wagon. The team would be taken from the wagon when they reached the area, then hitched to a Hercules Stump Puller to remove the pine stumps from the earth. The stumps would be loaded onto the wagons and taken to the turpentine plant, where they would be distilled in the large furnaces, producing pure, unadulterated turpentine from the pine pitch that remained in the stumps. When it became too expensive and too far to go for the pine stumps that remained after the lumbering days, the turpentine plant closed and its equipment was dismantled. The retort furnaces became culverts in the township roads where needed. These tubes were five feet in diameter, so I could walk through them when fishing without having to get out of the stream to go over to the other side of the road and back into the stream.

I had daydreamed back some years while standing there on the road looking upstream, and now I was ready to go fishing in earnest, until I came to the edge of the stream on the left bank where the ground was carpeted with princess pines. I was bent over and was carrying my fly rod backwards through the cover, for it is difficult to try to steer a fly rod head-first in dense undergrowth. Moving along slowly so that I could pick the good trout holes where the sun would not cast my shadow in the stream, I suddenly heard a loud whirring of wings and a blood-curdling, screeching sound that sent chills up my spine. An adult grouse hen madly flew into my old felt hat. I dropped my fly rod as I saw the princess pines before me quake rapidly, then grow still. I knew then that the grouse had a brood of babies. She had gone only a few feet and angrily returned, hitting me in the chest and

screeching. The third time she flew at my chest, I caught her in my hands and gently stroked her back until she calmed down completely. When she was quiet, I gradually released my hold on her, and she flew across the stream to a point from which she could watch me and still keep an eye on the place where her brood was hidden.

I cautiously moved ahead after picking up my fly rod, and, skirting the area where I felt the brood was hiding, took up a position behind a huge white pine stump near the stream, where I could watch, unseen, both the mama grouse and the spot where the brood was hidden. As I squatted down behind the stump, I stayed very quiet, for mama grouse seemed to know I was there. She screeched once but made no effort to attack me again.

Mama grouse was on an old dead cedar that was lodged in some other trees and extended over the stream. After about thirty minutes she had cooled down and felt it was safe to go to her brood.

This was a rather romantic experience for me, for I had trudged through these grouse woods since I was twelve, and this very spot was only one-and-a-half miles from where I had spent many hours in the grouse woods on the thousand acre Beaver Meadow Ranch in the southwest area of Ogemaw County.

Mama grouse puffed out her feathers a bit, walked to the end of the dead cedar and fluttered quietly off to where she had, in her own language, told her brood to hide and stay until she came back. She strutted over to the spot and in a quiet, low, clucking voice announced to her brood that she was there. Immediately, the little princess pines started quaking and the baby grouse appeared and joined their mama, single file behind her, as she strutted off through the underbrush.

Yes! I went on upstream and fished only the good, dark, deep holes and caught a nice mess of speckled trout. When I got home, I did not even tell my wife about the episode with the mama grouse for fear she would not believe it.

One day some years later, a friend, Ralph Chase, then from Traverse City, Michigan, stopped by our place and during the conversation told me and my wife of an experience that he had had the day before near his cottage, "The Gobblers Knob," on Bellew Lake. His story was a duplicate of the one I've just told, and it goes to prove that only a grouse hunter and a trout fisherman could understand the behavior of grouse.

My day on Perry's Creek in May 1935 was a delightful and educational one.

Moxie Crockett, dam of Fastrain and Card Shark.

Tools of the Trade

Listed below are the tools of a professional bird-dog trainer. An amateur, however, with one or two dogs to train will need only the specific tools his dog requires. All of these tools will be mentioned further and their uses described in the training sections of this book.

(1)   1/4-inch nylon cord leash with snap and hand loop.
(2)   18-inch steel stake with 2 1/2-inch ring-top "trainer's helper."
(3)   40-foot, 3/8-inch cotton sash cord with barrel snap.
(4)   3/4-inch dog collar with rectangular bell.
(5)   Roading harness with dee ring for drag chains. (Note: The ropes are inside of a piece of rubber hose.)
(6)   Sturdy leather 1-inch collar with end dee ring and nameplate.
(7)   Small-sized Acme Thunderer Whistle, Bakelite (not metal).
(8)   Leather pinch collar with 20-foot, 3/8-inch sash cord. (By making a knot every foot in the sash cord it becomes a stop cord, later illustrated.)
(9)   Tattletale Beeper Collar for Cover Dogs.
(10)   Two sponge-rubber balls on an adjustable 1/4-inch double nylon cord with snap (called an Equalizer).
(11)   15-foot, 3/8-inch sash cord with barrel snap.
(12)   .410 gauge hammerless single-barrel shotgun.
(13)   Leather holster for .22 and .32 blank pistols.
(14)   .22-caliber H&R blank pistol No. 9 shot.
(15)   .32 caliber H&R blank pistol No. 6 shot.

TOOLS OF THE TRADE.

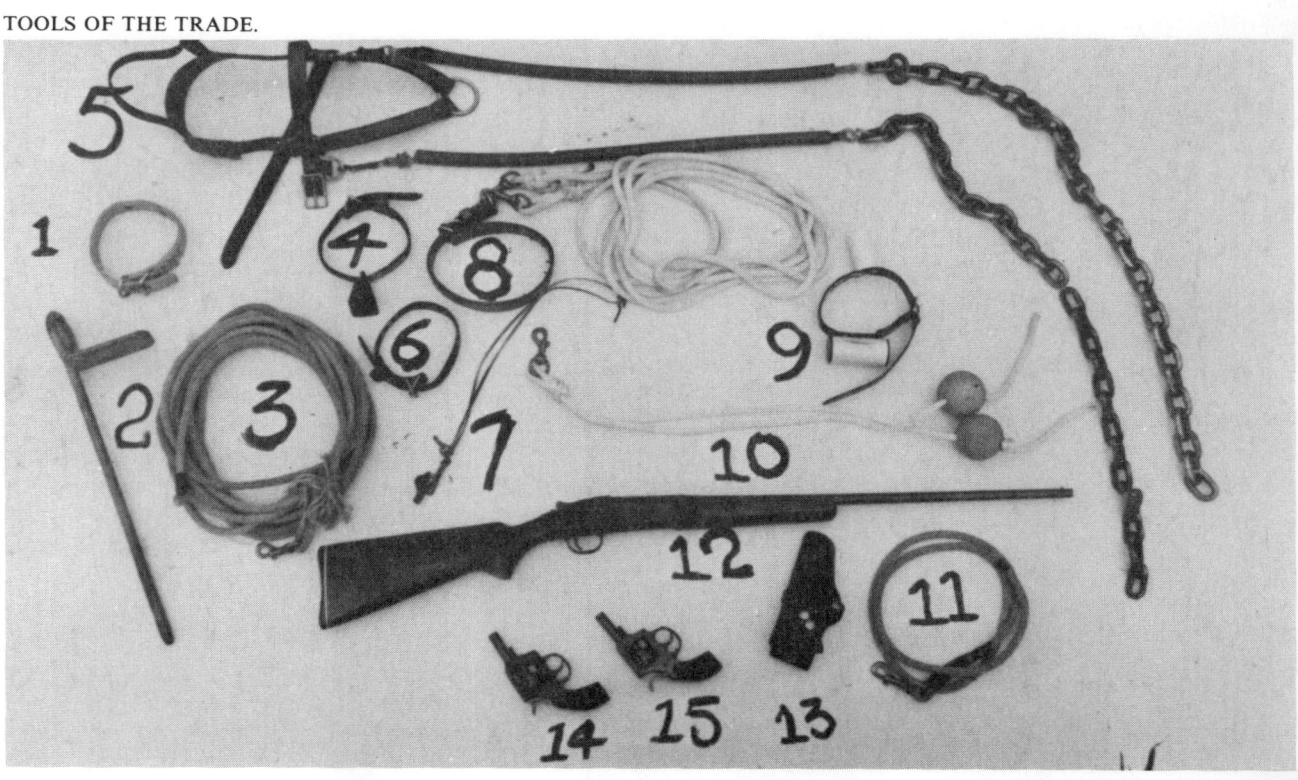

Teaching the dog to quarter,
turning to the front at the end of each cast.

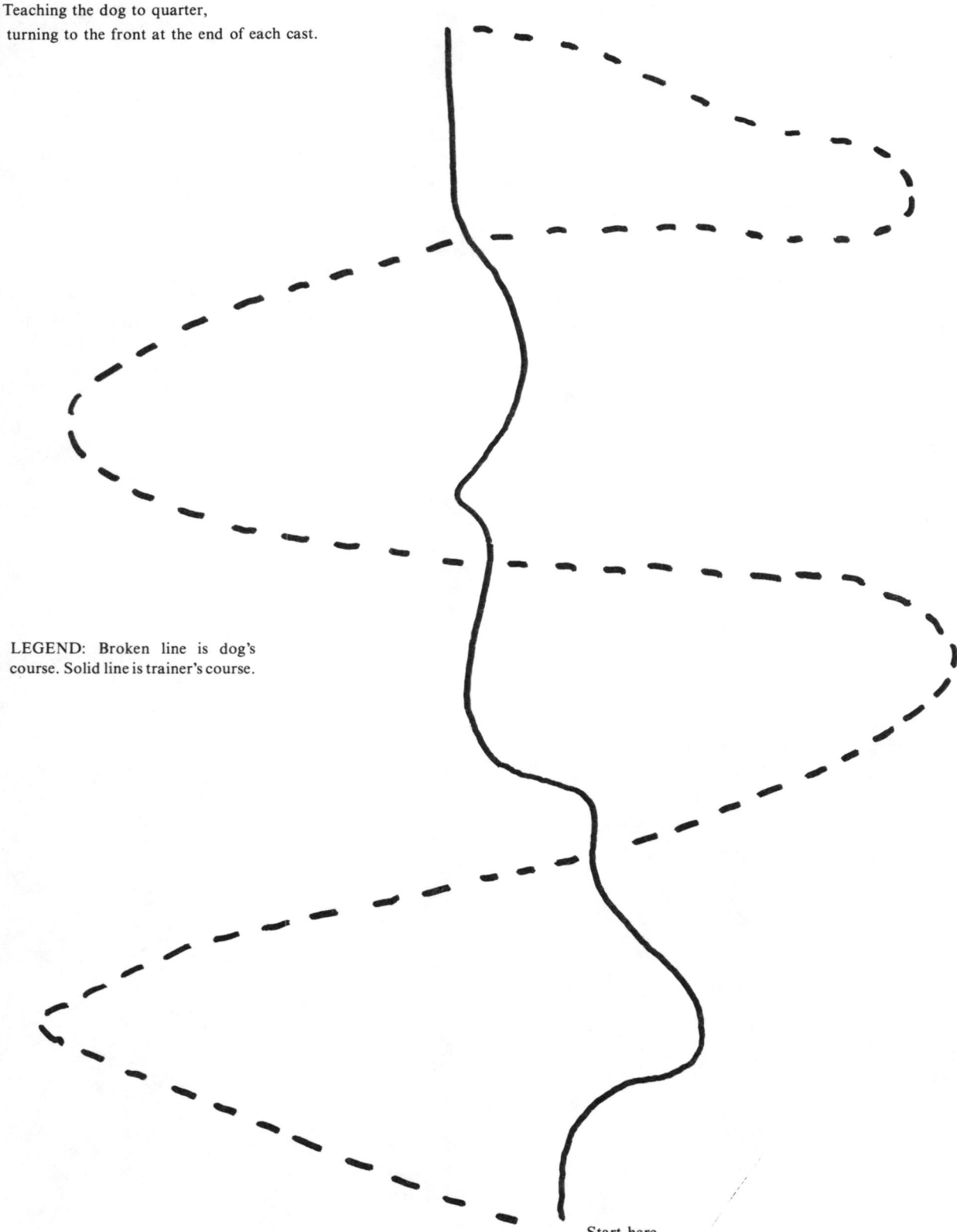

LEGEND: Broken line is dog's course. Solid line is trainer's course.

Start here.

Training Your Dog to Quarter

The chart on page 26 describes the course the trainer and dog take. A whistle is very effective here if the handler/trainer wishes to use a whistle rather than his voice alone. The dog can be started on two short toots on the whistle along with the term "head." When the dog is nearly as far to the left (see chart) as the handler/trainer desires, the handler/trainer moves gradually in the opposite direction, blows one long note on the whistle and repeats "head" to get the dog's attention. *Hand signals must not be used.* (See the chapter, "Why Not Hand Signals?") The handler/trainer will resume his straight-ahead general direction once the dog has started across in front of and to the right of the handler/trainer. The same system is used on the opposite side, as per the chart.

Besides learning to quarter, your dog will learn to respond to the whistle at the proper time and will learn what the word "head" means. Once he has learned to turn and go forward on one long note of the whistle, it is no longer necessary to say the word "head" each time you blow the one long note on the whistle. This is especially true when working in the grouse woods where the dog might not be visible. As the dog progresses, the two short toots on the whistle tell the dog he can go ahead.

Once the dog knows this, the knowledge can be very valuable in hunting grouse and woodcock—especially with a young dog, because there will be times when the dog points but indicates that he is not quite sure of the direction he is to go. Two toots on the whistle will release him to go on. Naturally, if the dog moves forward and puts up a bird, you should correct him immediately by bringing him back to where he originally pointed. Make him stand there four or five minutes and shoot over him, insisting that he stand to shot. This is all part of the process to produce a well-trained bird dog.

Why Not Hand Signals?

Hand signals to teach a grouse dog how and where to run and hunt are trouble-causing gestures on the part of the handler/trainer. The dog does not become an independent hunter, because it stops before completing each cast to look to its handler/trainer for instructions. The term "an independent hunter" does not mean a dog that goes off to hunt by himself, only showing up occasionally, then taking off again. The term means that a dog that is able to use its own initiative will learn quickly to be a productive hunter.

Too much yard training and the over-use of hand signals only disturb the dog, causing it to become too mechanical. Remember that, if the dog's ancestors are top-notch hunting stock, the dog knows more about bird hunting than the handler/trainer does. The dog enjoys the legwork while searching for grouse and woodcock. The handler/trainer should enjoy the dog.

Playtime before a yard work session. Photo by Wally Brzenk.

Teaching a young dog to heel. Photo by Wally Brzenk.

How to Yard Train Your Dog

There are three stages of yard training. The first stage is kindergarten, a kind of pre-school education to develop further the puppy's basic knowledge, such as learning its name, or coming to voice or whistle at feeding time. The puppy can also be taught to come by using a light check cord (one-quarter-inch nylon). Tie a bowline loop in one end, slip the other end of the cord through the loop and draw it up until the loop or noose will go just over the puppy's head. Do not jerk on the cord. Let the puppy fight it by himself. Once he discovers that he cannot run away from the situation, he will quiet down. Important— *do not talk*—say absolutely nothing while the puppy is xperiencing this ordeal. When the puppy has quieted !own, squat down or go down on one knee, draw up the slack in the check cord, and say "come" or "here"; at the same time pull on the cord—do not jerk. Just keep taking up the slack as the puppy comes. Once he has come to you, praise him. Most dogs, as time and their training progresses, learn both "come" and "here" as well as the two words together, "come here."

Letting the young puppy jump on you, at least when it is very young, three to five months of age, is acceptable, for it builds confidence and rapport. One important "don't"—don't let anyone scratch the puppy on the belly, for this will encourage the puppy to get on its back, and it will do so every time correction is necessary for any reason during later training. This a very bad habit and a difficult one to cope with.

Once the puppy is five to six months old, it can be taught by two methods not to jump up on you. As the puppy jumps up, step gently but firmly on one of his hind feet; at the same time, say "down." A few applications of this procedure and the puppy will know the difference between jumping on a person and the command "down." However, if the puppy is very bold, with a "devil-may-care" attitude, and comes running in hard to jump on you, just before he reaches you, on his way up, catch him in the chest with your knee and say "down." It is not necessary to knock the puppy over when doing this, only to stop him from coming up on you. This latter method works quickly. Once he is down, pat him. This way he learns that he can jump up on you when you permit but must stay down when told.

The second stage of yard work can start by the time the first stage is completed—at six months or a little older. The following steps should be taken one at a time at first. The best results are obtained in an enclosure—even the basement of your home works well. Before starting the training session, let the puppy have his short playtime until he settles down.

When teaching the dog to heel, it is important for the trainer to take into consideration beforehand whether he is a right- or left-handed gunner. Normally most dogs are taught to heel on the left side of the handler/trainer because most people shoot from the right shoulder. However, if the gunner who is going to be hunting this dog shoots from the left, the dog should be taught to heel on the right side. Why? When the gunner chooses to heel the dog for any reason while hunting, the dog should heel on the side opposite from the side on which the gunner is carrying his shotgun on his arm; if not, the gunner could trip or stumble, startle the dog, possibly discharge his gun, and accidentally shoot his dog.

On whichever side you choose to teach the dog to heel, the method is the same. The instructions given here are for training the dog to heel on the left. To train the dog to heel on the right, simply substitute right for left and left for right in the instructions which follow.

Have a good, sturdy, leather collar on the dog and a ten- to fifteen-foot, three-eighths to one-half-inch check cord. With the cord snapped onto the dog's collar, grasp the cord near the dog's collar with the left hand and hold the remainder of the cord coiled in the right hand, leaving only enough of the end of the cord to be twirled in front of the dog in a circular motion. Keep the loose end of the cord long enough to catch the dog under the muzzle but not so long that it will go around his head and strike him in the eye. Watch the dog closely. As he tries to step ahead, just before the cord catches him under the muzzle, say "heel." This lesson at first should be no longer than ten minutes duration. After two to three sessions, depending on the dog, it will be apparent that the dog has learned the term "heel"; however, he will, if he sees the chance to disobey, take advantage of you.

Two things can be done to instill the heel command thoroughly. Heel the dog close by his open kennel gate or his doghouse. He will make a dash to get in. Use the check cord to pull him up short, then circle around and again heel him close by the gate or doghouse. Repeat the procedure until he heels without your having to hold the check cord.

The second method works well if you are working only one dog, especially if the dog is an eager eater. This method is doubly rewarding if you work the dog before you feed him. Mix the dog's dinner and set it out in the yard where you will work the dog to heel. Heel the dog, with his paraphernalia on him, past the pan of food. As he makes a dash for the food, stop him short with the check cord. Circle around as many times as necessary past the pan of food until he will heel by the food without your holding the check cord.

The next step in yard training is teaching the command "whoa," but before starting to teach it, first put the dog through a short heel lesson. Hold the check cord about a foot from the dog's collar. While walking with the dog at your side, say "whoa," and pull up on the cord quickly, stopping the dog. Stand long enough so that the dog learns to stand still. Do this over and over until the dog stops the instant he hears you say the word "whoa" and without your pulling up on his collar with the check cord.

Important—keep your cool. Do not scream or yell at the dog during these lessons. Speak the command softly but firmly. It is not how loud you speak but what you do in teaching when the soft command is given.

Once the dog stops on the word "whoa," move one step to the side. Keep the cord in your hand. Then move another step to the side. If the dog moves from the whoa position, put him back in the same spot and start again, taking steps to the side. When you can take four or five steps to the side while the dog remains standing, then

Teaching a dog to whoa as he is coming toward the trainer. The trainer lets the dog go around the whoa post while holding on to the check cord, faces the dog, holds up his left hand, and says "Whoa" while holding the check cord tight, stopping the dog. Photo by Wally Brzenk.

Repeat the operation shown in photo at left at every yard work session, until you can drop the check cord and walk to your dog while he stays where he was whoaed. Photo by Wally Brzenk.

Trainer walking back to dog after the dog has been ordered to whoa. Photo by Wally Brzenk.

For good rapport between master/trainer and his dog, a little affection is all that is required. Kindness does help. Photo by Wally Brzenk.

move forward, a step at a time, watching the dog constantly. If he moves, put him back in the same spot and start again.

The object of walking several steps in front of the dog after first stepping to the side is to help the dog learn to remain on point while you are attempting to flush the bird. If the dog appears to want to move from his pointing position while you are trying to flush, the command "whoa" is in order.

Once these two steps are accomplished, the dog can be worked on the "whoa post." For this a longer check cord, forty to fifty feet long, and a pinch collar (with the points of the studs filed round) should be the training equipment. With the longer cord and regular or pinch collar, make two or three rounds with heel and whoa, then walk around the whoa post so that the dog is on one side, and you are on the opposite side. Whoa the dog, walk out in front of him but hold onto the check cord. Call the dog to come towards you. When he has come a short distance, say "whoa," snubbing the check cord quickly. This is to teach the dog to whoa or stop as he is coming towards the trainer. The trainer can hold his free hand up high as he issues this command. This gesture has a good effect later on as the trainer raises his blank pistol to shoot, for the dog has a tendency to tie it in with his whoa-post training. The whoa-post training should be of short duration—not more than five minutes—but every day, sometimes two or three times a day, until he has grasped the situation. Also, with each session, do not let the dog come all the way to you; rather, walk to the dog once he has stopped. Praise him, walk him around the yard at heel, then back to the whoa post. Having the whoa-post training down pat is very rewarding later on in advanced training.

Absolute Don'ts

—Don't chastise a dog under one year old.
—Don't chastise an overheated dog.
—Don't chastise a fatigued dog.
—Don't touch the dog if you are angry.

Cool off. If you cannot control yourself, you cannot control the dog. Ignoring this "don't" could make a good dog become a confirmed "blinker."

—Don't throw an overheated dog into a cold stream or deep pool.

All the nerves from the dog's brain follow the spine, and, if a dog is in cold water over its back, the shock damage to the dog can result in its death within a few days. Let the dog enter the stream by himself. As an example of what can happen, in the fall of 1948, Earl Gilliam went with me to the Upper Peninsula of Michigan for a few days' grouse hunting early in October. It was extremely hot one day while we were hunting with two Setters, my Smokey, nearly all black, and Earl's Pal, all white with a little orange on his ears. We had gotten into a goodly number of grouse at the very start of the hunt. As we followed up some of the grouse in various directions, an hour or so later, we discovered that we had lost our bearings, making it necessary for us to study the situation. Knowing that my truck was left at the side of a road east of the Griggs River, I told Earl, "We'll check our compass, pick out an object straight west, and keep going in this direction until we come to the Griggs River. Then we can follow the river south to the road where the truck is parked."

The dogs were very hot and had shortened their casts considerably. After three or four checks of the compass, we came rather abruptly to the Griggs River. There was a huge bend in the river where the water swirled around in a deep pool. Before I could stop Earl, he had picked Pal up and thrown him head first into that swirling pool of cold trout water. Smokey went to the river's edge and slowly waded out, lapping a drink on his way to cool off.

Pal finally came out of the pool, staggering, then fell. After a good rest we started hunting down river. In a hundred feet or so, Pal went into convulsions. After Pal recovered from the seizure, Earl kept him at heel. We did not hunt him the rest of the trip.

After getting back to my home in the Lower Peninsula, I received a phone call from a man in North Carolina. He wanted a finished grouse dog. I had none at the time, so I referred him to Earl Gilliam. They made a deal on Pal. The dog was shipped. A week after the man had received Pal, he called Earl, telling him the dog did not act quite right. The following week the man called Earl again, saying that Pal had died. No doubt he had received much nerve damage from the shock when thrown into the Griggs River.

Gun-Shy Dogs

Dogs are not born gun-shy. Gun-shyness is usually a man-made condition caused through foolishness or by accident. There are various degrees of gun-shyness. The most serious, of course, is when the dog runs off and hides when the shot is fired.

There is another type of gun-shyness that is not quite so serious. If not handled properly, however, it can become a downright nuisance. With this type, the dog wants to point birds, but, when the first shot is fired, the dog comes to the handler and walks along beside him and quits hunting. There are professional trainers who specialize in curing gun-shy dogs, but this type of gun-shyness is not too difficult to overcome if you will do the following: After the shot, when the dog comes to you, keep right on walking as if you are hunting. Completely ignore the dog. By all means, do not talk to the dog or show any sign that you feel sorry for him; this only adds injury to misery. Once the dog decides the shooting did not bother you, that you have gone on with "business as usual," the dog will hunt again. If you follow this practice each time the dog quits, he will hang around for a shorter length of time after each shot until finally he will not quit hunting at all, but stay out front hunting. Once the dog goes for the dead bird, the problem is cured.

Helpful Suggestions

One day, I finally figured out what to do about one end of my boot laces getting longer than the other end from day to day as I laced up my boots. It is simple. Remove the lace from the boot, tie a knot in the center, put the lace back in the boot so that the knot is between the two bottom eyelets, and the laces will remain even as long as they last.

Good boots that are quiet are the type with rubber bottoms that have a chain-type tread and leather uppers—excellent against dampness, and lightweight in the eight-inch height. They can be worn all day provided a shearling wool-type, steel-shank arch-support insole is placed in the boot to support the arch of the foot.

All-leather boots, eight inches high, are not too heavy and, if well-treated against moisture, will provide foot comfort for the person hunting grouse.

When shooting birds for your dog during training sessions, the best safety precaution is to use an inexpensive .410 gauge single-barrel, hammer or hammerless, shotgun. Paint the stock hunters' orange or bright red. After shooting the bird, the handler/trainer may wish to correct the dog; if so, he can put down the unloaded gun. The brightly painted stock enables the handler/trainer to see the gun once the dog has been corrected.

Jealousy is a great convincer, as you will learn from some of the short stories in this book. This is true where two male dogs are involved, or two bitches. One of the two always feels it is entitled to more of everything—affection, leeway, food, and so forth, which causes the other dog to do its best to get into the act. The handler/trainer should share equally with each of the dogs even though their jealousy shows, so that the two dogs will learn to wait their turn. This way they will not resort to fighting each other for the top spot with the handler/trainer. Dogs can be and should be taught to respect each other.

The current vermifuges for dogs are not usually as toxic as some in the past. However, if, after you treat a dog for worms, he develops the blind staggers or falls down, get one-half-cup of dark Karo Syrup down the dog as quickly as possible. In five minutes or so, the toxic condition will be neutralized.

For people who hunt their dogs in areas where porcupines are likely to be present, hemostats, or long, small-nosed pliers, are convenient for removing the quills. Also have handy a small bottle of vinegar. In cases where there is an abundance of quills in the dog, pouring the vinegar on them will help to soften the quills. If you do not have these items on hand, the quills can be pulled by bending them over the backside of an ordinary pocketknife blade. If the quills are exposed enough, it helps if the tip is cut off, thus allowing the hollow quill to collapse. Once the air is out, the quill can be removed more easily from the dog.

All-leather eight-inch boots, well treated for moisture, with rough soles, are good field and woodland footwear for grouse hunters. Photo by Wally Brzenk.

Rubber bottom footwear with leather uppers are great for grouse hunting if worn with steel shank insoles. Note the knot in the center between first eyelets. Photo by Wally Brzenk.

There is a right way and a wrong way to attach a harness snap to a dog's collar. If attached the wrong way, the dog may turn so that the thumb button on the snap will catch on the edge of the buckle in such an easy manner that the snap will fall loose from the dee ring on the collar, allowing the dog to go free. Always fasten the harness snap on the dee ring of the dog's collar with the gooseneck (opposite side of the thumb button) towards the buckle. This will prevent the dee ring from becoming detached accidentally.

Grouse dogs that work in briars occasionally will get an ear split, which will bleed profusely. A small bottle of "Newskin" often helps this condition.

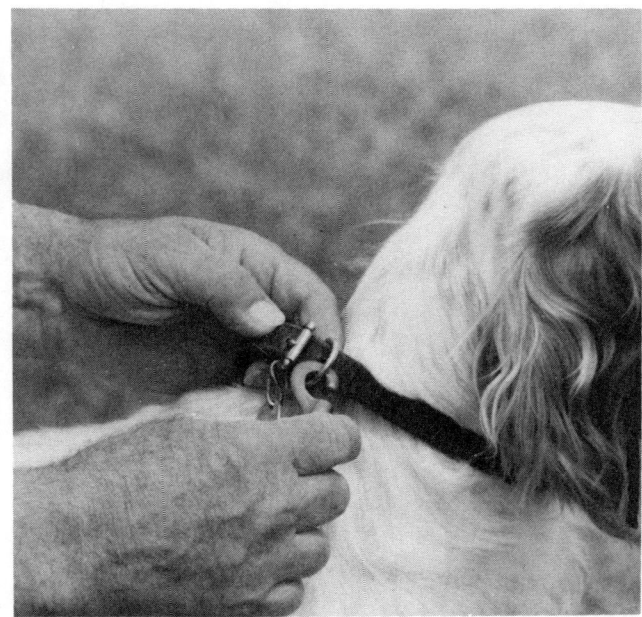
The right way to attach a harness snap to a dog's collar. Photo by Wally Brzenk.

The wrong way to attach a harness snap to a dog's collar. Photo by Wally Brzenk.
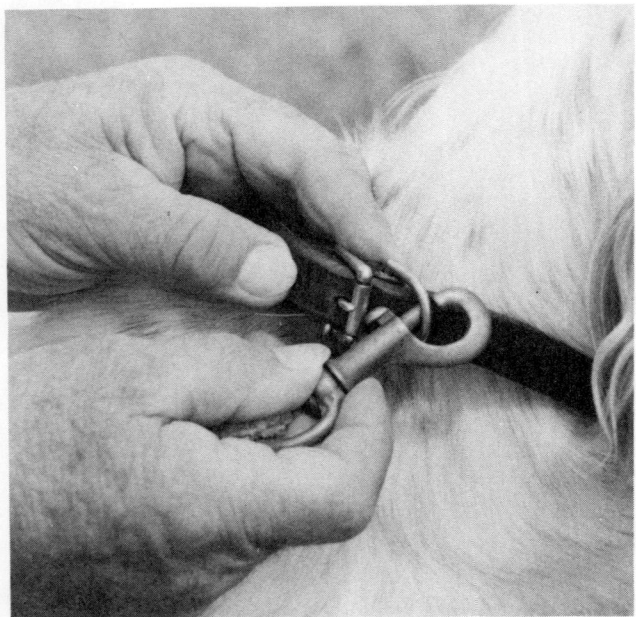

Don't Expect Too Much From a Puppy

It is easy to expect more from a seven- to fourteen-month-old puppy than you have a right to. True, some puppies come along faster than others. If the pup shows natural pointing instinct and searches, and at the same time makes some sensible effort to handle, you have the makings of a good gun dog.

People have come to me saying, "My new puppy is nothing like my old dog." They seem to forget what the old dog did at the same age, if they got him when he was a puppy. I have had puppies that, at one year of age, did work almost like an old dog—search, handle well, and point solidly as a rock. The next season when the dog becomes a year older—Oh, boy! Look out! It is known that a dog at one year of age is equivalent to a child of seven years. So now your puppy has become a Derby-age dog of two years, equivalent to a boy of fourteen going into high school. The boy tries to grow up quickly. He thinks he knows it all. So does that two-year-old dog of yours. This is known as the adolescent age. Really, this is not bad, since it shows spirit in your young dog. Stay with him; don't let up now on your previous yard work. Now is when it will start paying off on your hunting trips.

One time at a grouse trial a man in his late twenties walked up to me and asked, "Are you going South this winter to your winter training quarters?"

"Yes, we leave on November fifteenth," I answered.

"I have a seven-month-old Skylight Doctor pup I would like you to take South with you," he said.

About three days before we were to leave for the South, the man, his wife, and their little girl, about seven years old, arrived in our yard with the puppy.

"Do you have a place where we can turn him loose so that you can see what he does?" the man asked.

I replied that a field back yonder had some quail in it and that we could run him there.

We went back to the field and turned the puppy loose. He ran with a nice punchy gait, high head, and high, cracking tail; he really looked good. The puppy ran by a quail, and, as he slowed a little, the quail flushed. The puppy took after it for some distance.

"Look at that fool pup. He won't point but only chases birds," the man said.

The puppy soon crossed in front of us, flash-pointed a second quail, routed it out and gave it a really good chase. Although the man's remarks gave the impression that he was very disgruntled over the pup's performance, I really thought he was just pulling my leg until, when we got back to the kennel, he asked, "How long will you be down South?"

"Four months," I replied.

"Will my pup be steady to wing and shot, stop to flush, back another dog, and retrieve, when you get back in the spring?" he queried.

I knew then that the man was not pulling my leg. He was too serious. Standing there in amazement, I couldn't believe my ears. After regaining my composure, I asked, "Does your little girl go to school?"

"Yes, she does," he answered.

"Did you start her in the ninth grade?" I asked.

"Of course not. She started in kindergarten," he replied.

I didn't really want to sound absurd, so I said, "No offense, but you are asking me to take a nice puppy that should be in kindergarten, bring him back in four months a college graduate with a doctor's degree so that he can point staunchly, back another dog, is steady to wing and shot, and will stop to flush, and will retrieve on command."

No, I did not take that good puppy South.

That good puppy.

The adolescent age.

Brittany Champion Ban Dee. Mosseller Photography.

Types of Grouse Hunters and Their Dogs

There are probably as many different types of grouse hunters as there are different breeds of pointing dogs. There are some pointing breeds that are thought to be all-around dogs, even bred as all-around dogs in the beginning. Some of these dogs trail birds slowly more often than at a faster gait. A high-headed dog depends on the air current which carries the bird scent to its nostrils, and this in turn triggers their brain to do what they have been bred for, and that is to stop cold and point. Of all pointing breeds of grouse dogs, there are three—Setters, Pointers and Brittanys—that are specialists in the field of grouse and woodcock hunting.

The style of the person hunting often has much to do with the way his dog hunts grouse and woodcock. The person who hunts with a slow, trailing-type dog follows it closely to be near when the dog actually comes to point. Some people are productive hunting grouse and woodcock in this manner.

However, there is the person who takes his sport in another manner. He hunts with a high-headed, merry-tailed specialist that really handles well, but has the intelligence and bird sense to go over a hill, point a grouse or woodcock anywhere from a hundred to two hundred yards from his handler/trainer, and is staunch on point. This team will gain, in a productive way, over the long run, as much in game as the other type of handler and his dog. This latter style will produce game his handler would never know was in the vicinity if he were hunting with a closer dog that never gets out of gun range.

It appears that one man's "fancy" is another man's "folly." What counts is the results at the end of the day or hunting trip. It all boils down to what the Irish lady said when she kissed the cow: "Everybody to their own taste."

Tobacco River Zoe, by Tobacco River Bill ex Hobo's Lady, pointing grouse. Zoe is a high-headed winder.

Star, a Deutsch-Drahthaar, German Wirehaired Pointer.

Pirate, son of Tobacco River Bill, pointing a woodcock near Stapleton, Alabama.

Charlie Head's Setter Old Jake and Tobacco River Bill in Alabama

When I was training dogs in Alabama during the winters, a friend, Charlie Head, called me one day and said, "Let's go quail hunting. You bring Tobacco River Bill, and I'll meet you at the Echo Drive-In. We'll go in the afternoon." I saw Charlie's pickup parked at the drive-in when I arrived at noon. Old Jake was in the back end of the pickup. Old Jake was a ten-year-old white-and-chestnut Setter. After having a quick lunch, we left to go out on the Bromley Road. Charlie had said that he had seen woodcock out there in the past few days while he was cruising the timberland.

Shortly after getting on the Bromley Road, we pulled off into a field across a ditch. Old Jake was still in the back end of the truck, and I was riding with Charlie in the front with Bill on the floor. As we crossed the ditch going into the field, Charlie stopped. I let Bill out, and he stood right beside the truck pointing. As I looked back, Old Jake was standing on the tailgate of the pickup pointing towards the ditch. Charlie and I got out of the truck, loaded our shotguns, and went in front of the dogs toward the ditch. A large covey of quail arose, flying across the road into a piney thicket. Charlie dropped two birds and Old Jake retrieved both birds. I wasn't letting Bill retrieve at the time, although he would have. Right after hunting the thicket for awhile, we found several birds but could not get any shooting; the underbrush was just too thick. So Charlie said we should get out of there and go up the road to hunt on the north side of the road, which we did. After about five minutes on the north side of the Bromley Road, my Bill pointed. Jake was standing off on the right backing; for both dogs—very pretty work. I said to Charlie, "You flush the bird." Charlie went in; a woodcock flushed and he shot it. He spent several minutes looking for it. Both dogs were standing.

"If you don't find it pretty soon, I'll let Bill go and retrieve it," I said.

With that, Charlie said, "Well, Old Jake won't retrieve a woodcock; he won't point one either. He has never pointed one in all his life, and he has never retrieved one."

After Charlie searched for the bird for two or three minutes and couldn't find it, I tapped Bill on the head and said, "Dead bird, Bill—fetch!" He ran over there and picked it up, bringing the bird to me.

After hunting all of that side and going to the west and hunting the north side of Bromley Road, we found no quail. But we were getting into woodcock, one right after another. Bill had twenty-three finds on woodcock in about an hour and a half with Old Jake backing every time, just as pretty as could be, and Charlie shooting some birds. He'd retrieve most of the birds himself. Occasionally, I'd have to let Bill retrieve one that he couldn't find, and Jake would watch.

It was about 3:30 in the afternoon, and we crossed over the Bromley Road back on the south side, since we were hunting our way back to where the truck was parked on the north side of the road. As we were going along, Bill found two or three more woodcock and Jake would get in a little closer, each time backing, but he always backed very beautifully. I think maybe we killed one or two birds on that side of the road, and, as we crossed the road and got on the other side, I looked up and saw Jake pointing. That's right; you guessed it. He was pointing a woodcock—his first and his last. Jake was ten years old. Not only did he point it; Charlie killed it, and Jake retrieved the bird, too. So you can see that an old dog can learn new tricks from a young dog.

Jake was a trailing-type dog on quail. He trailed birds; he would trail them from last week's trail, I believe. Sometimes I think he was doing just that, because it would take him some time to locate a covey of birds, but he would stay with them.

As we were headed towards the pickup, which was parked about a quarter of a mile back in the woods, Charlie said, "There's Old Jake over there," and there he was, trailing some birds along the ground. Just about that time, Charlie looked up and saw Bill running way off to the right, and he said to Jake, "You'd better get out of there. That white dog is going to get up there and find those birds before you even know about it." About that time Bill pointed about seventy-five yards out in front—straight up. Old Jake backed him and, wouldn't you know, that big covey of birds flew straight towards Charlie's pickup. We couldn't get a shot, not a one. So, as I said before, an old dog can learn new tricks from a young dog.

What Is a Good Pheasant Dog?

A good pheasant dog is one that works fast and hard. It isn't necessary for him to be "right under your feet"; that is, close. When the dog hits his bird hard on point, and then, as you walk to him, he flags the uppermost end of his tail erratically, he is telling you that the bird is moving or running off. When he signals in this manner, tell him to go on (get out of there). If he charges straight in, flushing the bird, catch him quickly, place his ear on the nameplate of his collar, then press his ear against the nameplate with your thumbnail, while walking him back to the spot where he pointed. Just as you approach that spot, release all pressure on his ear. This is very important because a dog should never be chastised at the spot where he pointed; rather, when you reach the spot, stand him in a pointing position and talk softly to him, stroking him at the same time. By doing this you and the dog will be on equal terms when you send him on. Besides, after a few episodes of the above, the dog will learn to break point and then run swiftly around and ahead of the running bird. Subsequently, he will whirl and pin the bird hard and intensely. In every case, the bird will be from three to four feet from the pointing dog, sitting tight, completely mesmerized.

When you are hunting pheasant with your dog and he indicates that game is nearby, do not talk to him too much. This is one of the mistakes many handlers make, and this applies to just about every game bird you might be hunting. The dog listens to you instead of doing his job independently.

Which reminds me of the time a man I never saw before walked into my kennel near Saginaw, Michigan. As he walked through the kennel, he remarked, "Humph—field trial dogs! I have a Setter at home that will find more birds than all seven of these Setters put together."

With that, I introduced myself, saying to the stranger, "I like a good bird dog, and I'm always happy for a man who has one."

This man stopped by our kennel several times within a couple of weeks, each time having some snide remark to make about my dogs. I was beginning to get somewhat irked. It has often been said, "You can talk about my wife, but don't talk about my dog."

It was along about September, and, as this man was leaving, I said, "I'll tell you what. I'll be free tomorrow about six-thirty in the evening. You bring your dog here, and I'll take one of mine and we'll go to a place where there are some pheasants."

"Okay, I'll do that," he replied.

The man showed up the next evening on time with his Setter. It was a beautiful dog. I brought my Direct Heirs Rodfield. He was twenty-six months old and had developed into an extremely good pheasant dog.

We took our dogs south along the Dixie Highway between Saginaw and Bridgeport where I had permission to work my dogs. As we approached the eighty-acre hayfield, I said, "Since you have more or less challenged me and my dog, you can run your dog first." He thanked me and turned his dog loose. This Setter was all white with black ticks, had a very good conformation, and weighed about fifty pounds.

It did not take long to learn what the dog's name was. He had not gone more than fifty yards when he pointed, then started catwalking and pointing. The man kept repeating to the dog, "Whoa, Joe, easy, careful now." Then he would turn to me and say, "Isn't that beautiful?"

"Yes," I replied, "but you cannot eat those points. You have to produce a bird."

His dog worked in this fashion more than halfway down the field. Not once did the man ever get in front of the dog to flush a bird. Two pheasants flushed far ahead, far out of gun range. "There go Joe's birds," the man said. With that he heeled his dog back to my car.

I brought Rod out on a leash to the same field. The stranger said, "Why don't you go to another field to give your dog a fair chance? My dog found the only two birds in this field."

With that remark I turned Rod loose. He dashed to the left side of the field, running straight ahead along a fence towards the far end of the field. My friend yelled, "There goes your field-trial dog. He's running away."

"Let's watch him to see what he does," I remarked.

Nearing the end of the field, Rod turned quickly to his right, and stood head and tail high. Without a word we walked to the dog. I walked in front, and at about eight feet a huge cock pheasant took wing. I could have hit it with a stick, it rose so close to me. As we hunted our way back to my car, Rod had two more classic finds, handled as nicely as his first find.

What this man didn't realize was that Rod worked independently, without a word from me. Besides, he had bird sense, as evidenced by the fact that, because the wind was behind him, he ran to the far end of the field and worked back toward me.

The man did not say four words all the way home, nor did he ever tell me who he was. He never came to my kennel again.

Through the years I have had dog customers ask me what causes a smart pheasant dog to circle a bird. I like the term "relocate" rather than "circle" because the dog does not really circle the bird. He is smart enough to get far off to the side and outrun the bird. His nose tells him when he has the advantage over the bird, and he points hard and intensely.

Whenever a dog customer would ask me the above question, I'd ask him to play a little game with me. I'd say, "You be a cock pheasant; I'll be the dog." He would always agree, and we would have a go at it: It is early in the morning. You (the pheasant) have been roosting snugly in a hay field all night when suddenly you hear a rustling sound. You look up quickly and there I (the dog), am. You ease away in the opposite direction, skulking along under the alfalfa in order to stay out of sight, when all of a sudden you run right into me (the dog) again. You are not smart enough to know I am the same dog. You say to yourself "Holy cow! There is a dog back there where I roosted and now another one here. I'll just sit tight right here until they go away."

Most always my customers get a kick out of this little game, and it clarifies their question about a good pheasant dog's behavior on a running pheasant.

About scent: it travels like smoke from a small bonfire. As it gets farther away from the source, it spreads out, becoming much thinner and weaker. Dogs understand this better than we do. One reason dogs far off from a bird sometimes will appear uncertain is because the scent is spread out thinly.

A good pheasant dog.

Spot Hunting

Because I hunted grouse alone many times, I became a spot hunter, stopping off at likely places I knew well for a short hunt of a half-hour to an hour, then moving on a mile or so to another birdy-looking area. Some days I would work eight to ten areas. This way all three of the dogs with me would get ample work on grouse.

One particular trip I spent four days hunting in every direction from West Branch, Michigan, for a radius of ten miles, stopping off at good places just for short hunts from daylight until dark. There were times when fire could be seen belching from my gun barrel when the first bird lifted early in the morning and again when the last bird lifted in the evening. Those were the good old days when my legs were much younger and grouse more plentiful.

The third day of this particular hunt proved to be exciting and unusual. When I arrived southwest of West Branch, near the Beaver Meadow Ranch (now called the Long Timber Ranch), it was a bit frosty; so I did not start my hunt until the sun had released the frost from the ground foliage. This gave me a chance to map out a few hunts around the area, first on an abandoned farm and the forty acres of state land west of Charlie Post's farm, then around to the south and east along the old Hoffman Branch railroad grade. In the lumbering days when the railroad grades were built to haul logs from the forest, Swedish men were hired. These men, called "Swedes" for short, worked on either side of where the railroad grade was to be built and shoveled the dirt up from either side onto the grade, which was later leveled before the ties and rails were laid. The holes on the sides of the grade became known as "Swede holes." The Swede holes along each side and for some distance back from the grade had grown up to excellent grouse cover.

That morning I chose Jurex's Silver Lady to hunt with me. She proved to be a good choice since the grouse and woodcock lay tight. They seemed to be reluctant about leaving their hiding places; so the dog's bird work was extra good with positive locations on her birds.

By the time Lady and I reached the old Hoffman grade, we bagged two grouse and a woodcock. The grade was a comfortable place to hunt. The dog quartered back and forth across the grade, hunting both sides as deep as two hundred feet.

The first half-mile of the grade took us right up to Harry White's farm, where there were a few small pasture lots grown up to wild grasses. Just before reaching these lots, Lady pointed solidly on the left of the grade. Two grouse exploded as I approached the dog. The dense popple trees here made a double retrieve just about impossible, though I bagged one. A few minutes later, Lady pointed on the right of the grade along a small trout creek where I bagged a woodcock.

After Lady retrieved the woodcock, the unusual happened. At least it was unusual for Lady to disappear for any length of time unless she was on point. She had gone far to the right, where, by looking through the dense popples, I could see a yellowish grassy portion of a pasture lot. Not being able to locate Lady in the woods, I had to look in the grassy field. Lady had hunted many pheasant fields in the Saginaw Valley and was also an excellent pheasant dog.

When I reached the pasture lot, there stood Lady about seventy-five yards out in the grassy field, solid as a rock. Before I could flush, Lady broke point, ran about fifty feet and pointed again. This time I saw the culprit, a huge, ring-necked pheasant, just walking and squawking at each step. He was not frightened at all and seemingly had no intention of flying. I followed him several yards until I was close enough to get my foot under him and raise him into the air as high as my head. It seemed like the pheasant flew so slowly that he would never get far enough away to shoot him. Finally, I did shoot my 20 gauge with No. 8 shot, light loads, and that cock bird came down with a thud.

Lady had to bring him to me by one wing, he was so huge. This pheasant measured forty-nine inches from its beak to the end of its tail and weighed six pounds, three ounces on a fisherman's scale. When I was a boy growing up on the Beaver Meadow Ranch in 1918, the county agent gave me pheasant eggs, which were hatched under setting hens, raised until eight to ten weeks old, and then released in the grain fields. No doubt this lazy, over-sized cock pheasant was a relative.

It was Tuesday, my last day of the trip. I decided to cross the Rifle River east of West Branch, taking the second sand trail south toward Greenwood, where I could get back on the highway to my home in Saginaw. I had already filled my quota of woodcock for this trip but could have used three more grouse to make this hunt complete. With me in addition to my Setter Jurex's Silver Lady, were her daughter Silver Lady's Josephine, called "Jo," and her granddaughter Direct Heir's Dawn.

The first place I stopped was a popple area. The ground was covered with wintergreen, which was loaded with its red berries that year. Dawn went to work quickly, darting from one side to the other in front of me. I had decided to try to obtain one grouse for each dog. Crossing a small clearing into what might be termed a popple bluff of about three acres with a clearing all around it, Dawn pointed solidly just in from the edge. When the grouse flushed, it flew high to go over the trees. At the shot, it came down with a thump.

Dawn went to retrieve. Instead of picking up the bird, she pointed, which is something she rarely did when sent to retrieve. She was standing about two feet from the bird, which lay flat, with wings spread out, very dead, and close to a large popple. As I reached for the bird, Dawn dove in, grabbing it along with my hand, then rolled over on her side, still gripping the bird and my hand with a death grip. Believe me, it was painful. I thought the dog was dead. Slapping and shaking her with my left hand did no good; so I got down close and blew in her ear. When I said, "Let go," she gave up the bird. She stood up, staggering as she started to walk. I came to the conclusion that she had hit her head on the large popple when she dove in to get the bird. However, she recovered and she hunted well later when we were going back to the car.

Moving down the trail a mile or more, Lady and I took a fifteen-minute swing on the left side of the trail along a cedar swamp. Lady had two finds. It was a clean miss on the first, for the grouse made it to the swamp to be around for another time. The bird on the second find was not so fortunate.

As we drove down the sand trail, we came to a turn-off in the trail where someone had dumped tin cans and rolls of old fence wire. Since Jo was eager to get started, we circled the junk that had been dumped there and headed for a ridge that ran to the east.

After a forty-minute hunt in that direction, Jo and I turned back towards where the car was parked, without having seen a grouse. Because it was getting near noon, I planned to go home when we got back to the car. Nearing the end of this little hunt a short way from the car, Jo pointed towards that old roll of fencing. That's right; the grouse was in that roll of fencing. It flew straight down the sand trail where, at the shot, it dropped in the middle of the trail.

Everything loaded, we headed for home. I wonder why the trip home always seems shorter when you have a successful, productive hunting trip than when you go home empty-handed?

As I turned in the driveway, I realized my responsibility, because there sat my "first lady" on the front porch, dressed in a dark suit and white blouse with ruffles down the front, her golden hair glistening, but outshone by her happy smile as she embraced me when I stepped out of the car. That "first lady" was my wife, Ruth. After her affectionate greeting, she asked, "Did you have a good hunt, and how did the dogs do?" This was the end of a fabulous hunt. A hunter who can go on a hunt and come home to an understanding wife like Ruth is rich, indeed.

A Gordon Setter in the grouse woods.

Modern-Day Grouse

The thousand-acre stock ranch in the southwest corner of Ogemaw County where I went to live as a twelve-year-old boy who had never before seen wildlife, held many wonders for me: grouse, woodcock, deer, black bear, rabbits (cottontail and snowshoe hare), woodchuck, mink, weasel, and beaver. The wild land on this ranch had by then grown up with poplar (aspen) trees, wild pin cherry and chokecherry on the ridges, red and gray dogwood along the lowland, and white and red oak. The low areas had cedar, balsam swamps, and several small creeks (trout streams) throughout.

When I first started hunting game birds in this paradise, back in 1918, the grouse was king. Today he is even more a king. Why? In two words: "selective breeding." Grouse were the same birds then as they are today, but without the knowledge of man as an enemy or pursuer. When I would walk along the poplar and oak ridges along the sides of the swamps, I would often stumble right into what could be called a covey of fully grown grouse parading around unafraid. I would make a quick jump at them, sometimes as many as eight to fifteen birds. They would not fly, but merely jump a foot or two to one side or the other, making their usual little talk— "poot, poot, poot," probably trying to tell me, "Don't bother us. We are food hunting." Those were remarkable, entertaining days that provided me with a knowledge I could not get in the little red schoolhouse I attended some two miles from home.

I had no bird dog in those days. The grouse were not afraid of me and were my friends. They acted as if they expected me. Sometimes, as I came upon a covey feeding near the thorn apple or a ridge of oaks, I would sit on a nearby stump and watch the grouse feed and cavort around. As the years went by, I returned to these same grounds each fall to hunt, only to find that other men were hunting these same areas with their good bird dogs as well. These ruffed grouse, which up to then had not been afraid of man, were experiencing a new type of man with a four-legged companion. So what happened? The trusting young grouse that lingered there, flushed close by, were usually shot. The smart ones learned to run, evading the man and his dog and, therefore, surviving to produce smarter grouse.

As the years passed, the smarter grouse of each season learned to survive the depredations of man and his dog, as well as Nature's other predators, but man is the prime factor in this "selective breeding." The surviving grouse live on to maintain their status of king of all the game birds—the gorgeous, ruffed grouse.

King of the game birds: a Ruffed Grouse drumming.

Grouse Tactics

One beautiful October afternoon, the late Dr. C. Ford DeVries arrived to go grouse hunting with me on the Schmidt place north of Farwell, Michigan. The two dogs we hunted with were his Waverly Mike and my Kings' Chief General (Windy). As finished dogs, both were fast, wide, and stylish. Mike had not been hunted for a few days so he had his "running shoes" on. When the dogs were set loose to hunt, Mike disappeared to the right front and Windy went left along a creek. Ford and I walked leisurely along, more or less killing time as we waited for those two Setters to get their first head of steam worked off. As we approached a clearing near the top of the ridge, ten or twelve grouse rose from the deep June grass that surrounded a big white oak tree, flew straight ahead about a hundred feet, and lit in some hazel shrubs and bushes with large yellow leaves drooping from the branches. This could have been one brood that was raised in the area.

Since there was no dog involved, we did not shoot at the grouse, though we were close enough to do so. Turning to Ford, I said, "Let's not disturb those grouse now. We can go down the hill along the stream and hunt back as far as the Ann Arbor railroad, then work back, because I believe those grouse were feeding on acorns in that grass around that white oak tree." Just before reaching the railroad, we found Windy on point. The good doctor bagged a nice adult grouse for Windy, which he retrieved when told to do so. Windy was settling down to serious hunting. He also was a great front-hunting dog, never coming from the rear. The shooting for Windy's bird brought Mike in; so he too settled down. We were hunting back along the ridge that, in a few minutes, would bring us near the big oak tree from which the brood had flushed earlier. Straight ahead was Mike, standing high near the hazel shrubs where the grouse had flown. Approaching Mike, we found he was backing Windy, who was pointing towards the big oak tree.

Ford and I skirted the two dogs to get in a good position, since the land was open to the north of the big oak, so the birds would be in the open for fifty yards or so when they flushed. Ford was in an excellent position when the grouse started going out of the grass one and two at a time, flying out in the open. Ford bagged three grouse while I was busy bagging one and missing two.

When the shooting ceased, the two dogs did the honors of fetching our prize birds. On our way to the car Ford asked, "How did you know those grouse would go back under that oak tree after we left at the first flush when we came in the woods?"

"This time of day, late in the afternoon when grouse are feeding on choice food, they are reluctant to go far and will return to the food as soon as they feel the intruders have gone. This is especially true when dogs are not involved and no shooting has taken place," was my answer.

Nearing the car just before dusk, Ford thanked me for the hunt, saying, "This is the nicest afternoon grouse hunt I've had this season."

Tobacco River Crockett.

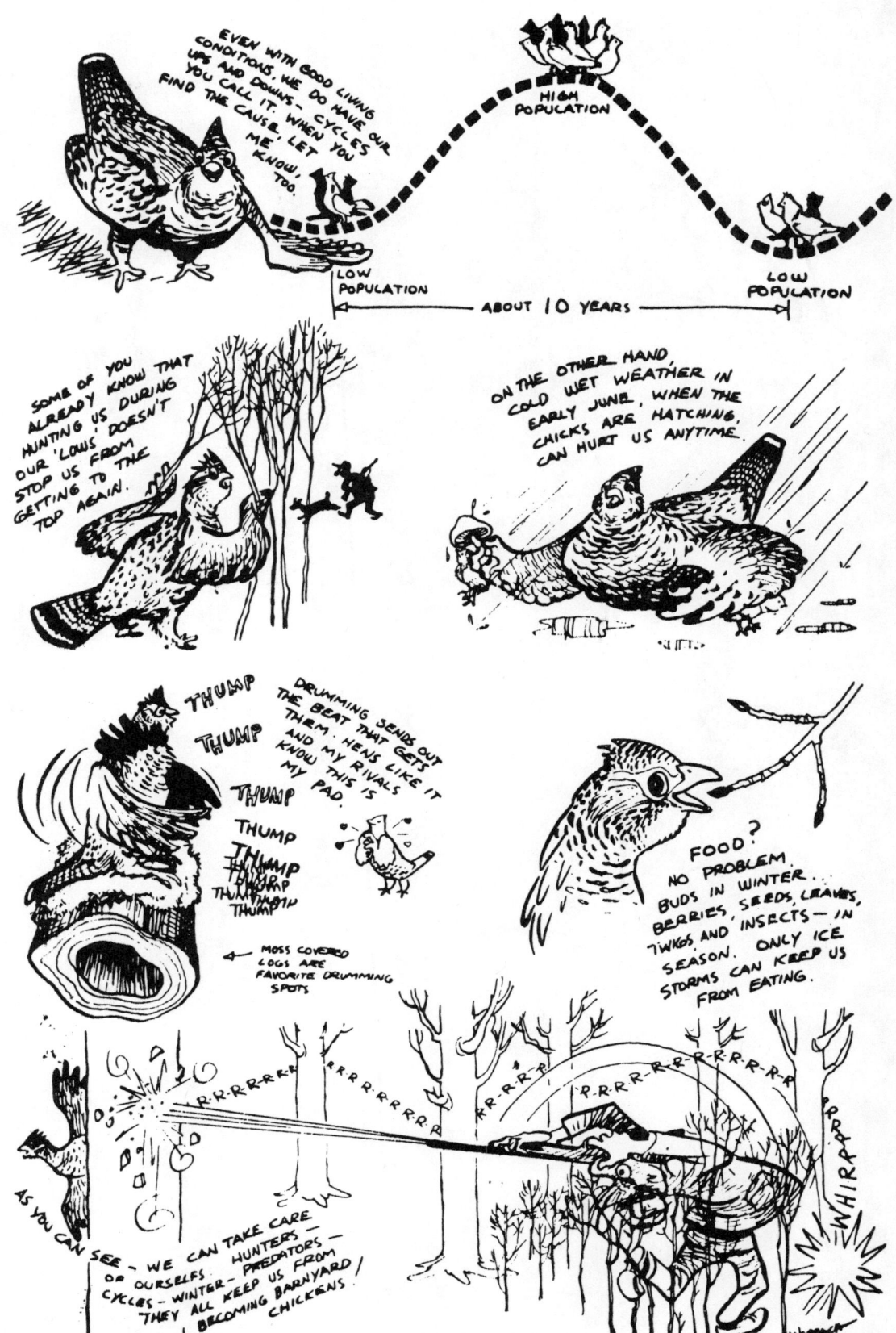

By Oz Warbach. Reprinted by permission of the Michigan Department of Natural Resources, formerly Michigan Department of Conservation.

Grouse Hugging White Pine Stumps

One fall day in 1964, while working Tobacco River Bill around a huge cranberry marsh on the side of the old Harrison Branch grade, a strange thing happened. We had been working for some time and were nearly all the way around the marsh when Bill's bell went silent some distance ahead. I soon found him standing in a low place, pointing straight ahead.

I stomped around through the high ferns and brush directly in front and to the sides, then told the dog to relocate. He refused to budge, maintaining his stylish intensity. So I went farther out front, back and forth several times around a huge white pine stump, without flushing a bird. When I tried again to send the dog on and he still refused, I took him by the collar and walked him off point some twenty-five yards. He immediately went back to the same spot, pointing as before.

This time I walked behind the dog, bent down, and sighted down his nose. There, about fifty feet ahead, a large grouse was clinging to the side of that huge white pine stump about three feet from the ground, with its wings spread flat, head and neck stretched, and tail hugging the stump as though it were frozen there. As I walked right up to the stump, the grouse never quivered. I believe I could have caught that grouse with my bare hands. Instead, I poked it with my hand, causing it to take to the air, then shot my blank pistol over the dog.

A similar thing happened just after the conclusion of the Grand National Grouse Futurity in Pennsylvania. The late Don Olson and I decided to go out after lunch to work Tobacco River Bill and Ghost Train. These two dogs were first- and second-year All-Ages. Don wanted to teach Ghost Train to back.

Lunch finished, we went out to the Buzzard Swamp road to where a good many quail had been released that morning for the Grouse Futurity second-series dogs. Shortly after turning Rusty (Ghost Train's call name) and Bill loose, Rusty pointed in a boggy area at the edge of a swamp and Bill came in and backed. Don flushed a quail. We then went to a higher and drier area of the sparse, small oak trees. Soon Bill pointed in an open place. Don called Rusty in and got him to back. I was unable to flush a bird. The dogs were both standing nicely; so Don tried to flush a bird for the dogs, without results. He became disgusted with Bill, saying to me, "Bill doesn't know what he's doing." Don took Rusty on. I finally took Bill away, sending him on. He made a wide circle to the left, going back to the same spot, and pointed with intensity. Again I could not flush a bird. Trying to get Bill to go was like trying to move a balky mule. Finally, I squatted down behind the dog, looking ahead toward a small six-inch-size oak tree. There was the quail, four feet up from the ground, clinging to the side of the tree.

By this time Don had gone on several hundred yards with Rusty. I left Bill standing while I went to get Don and Rusty to come. Eventually they came. Rusty backed Bill again. When I told Don to check the side of the oak tree, he could hardly believe it. "Never in my life have I seen anything like this. Do you suppose the bird is dead?" he said.

"Why don't you go and see?" I replied.

Don walked right up to the tree. He grasped the bird in his hand; the quail gave a kick and was off, flying away a good distance. On the way back to our dog wagon, Don kept exclaiming, "I'm glad you called me back to see that quail on the side of the oak tree, because I don't think I would have believed it had I not seen it."

Windy's Pride.

A Welcome Grouse-Hunting Invitation

After coming home from our training headquarters in the black belt farming region of Alabama one spring, Tobacco River Bill and I went to an area near our Farwell, Michigan, home known to the natives as "Slab Town." Much of this area is state land and very good cover for grouse and woodcock. The area is approxi—mately three square miles in size. There is some flat land covered with aspen, Juneberry, some birch, many evergreens such as balsam and white spruce, cedars along the swamps, dogwood and smaller evergreens growing around potholes, and now and then a huge proud white pine or red pine. Oh, yes, blackberry briars, too. Some of the area near the pond is rolling, serving as an excellent place to teach young grouse dogs to become woods-wise. Since we had arrived early in the morning and it was cool, bright, and sunny, I decided to work the north side of Slab Town through the aspen, pin cherry, chokecherry, and thorn apples, where some of the clearing had been planted with Austrian pine, which were now about six feet high.

It was early April, and the woods' greenery, such as the bracken, had not yet appeared. About the only ground cover was wintergreen. Bill, my Setter, had been down about fifteen minutes and was out front to my right some seventy-five yards when a grouse took wing from under a Juneberry shrub to the right of me and flew past me to my left. It flew only about six to eight feet high about a hundred yards and pitched in under an Austrian pine. As I stood watching it, Bill came in to check on me. When he reached the vicinity where the grouse had flushed from under the Juneberry shrub, he raised his head up high and ran as fast as he could right down the air scent of the flight of that grouse. About sixty feet from the pine where the bird had landed, he changed ends and stood both ends high on an intense point. Walking slowly to the dog and in front to flush, I couldn't help but notice how the dog's coat glistened in the sunlight. When the grouse flushed, Bill's eyes sparkled as he looked into the sun, watching the bird in flight. The shot from my blank pistol rang out as he stood where he had stopped. In my sixty years of grouse hunting, Bill was the second dog I had seen follow the air-scent flight of a grouse.

Another time we were hunting with August J. Neberle and Fletcher Carscallen, near Lupton, Michigan. They owned litter brother Laverack Setters: Dusty, an orange belton, owned by Fletcher, and Windy's Pride, a blue belton owned by Neb, as he is affectionately known by his close friends. Both were excellent grouse and woodcock dogs. Windy was the better retriever. Windy and Dusty came from Dr. C. Leeper of Cleveland, Ohio. The breeder was Stanley Kresina.

We were hunting two of my Setters, Jurex's Silver Lady and her granddaugher Direct Heir's Dawn, who, incidentally, is a great-granddaughter of Candy Kid. We had started hunting at daylight that morning. Normally, I hunted with only one other person, but Fletcher and Neb, being excellent grouse hunters, and I, having been the invited guest, all hunted well together. Neb informed me ahead of time that the hunt was going to be a long one that morning. Since there were no roads, it would all be a woods hunt, through and around potholes back near a lake. The dogs worked well, and the hunt was going along nicely. We had moved a goodly number of grouse that morning and bagged some, but found no woodcock.

About eleven o'clock, Neb said, "We'll swing around to the south and work our way back to your car, Jack, so we can arrive there around two o'clock. I have another place in mind for a late evening hunt with Dusty and Windy."

At about noon, we came to a nice sunny place under a big oak tree. It was an inviting place to have our sandwiches and then a short siesta. Lady and Dawn came in and lay down beside me. Before eating my sandwich and having a soft drink, I opened a can of dog meat with a small key-type can opener. This was the standard "long-hunt lunch" for both man and dog. Opening both ends of the can, I pushed the meat about halfway through the can for Lady, then pushed the balance out for Dawn. After eating, all of us, including the dogs, took a nap. Avid grouse hunters don't nap long when there are good dogs to watch in action, as well as grouse to be found, and we were soon on our way, hunting the ridges that ran alongside the tag alders.

Lady and Dawn had disappeared into the tag alders on our right some fifty yards ahead as we walked together on the ridge. When you are hunting with Mr. Neberle, you stay close together and let the dogs do the legwork. Lady was espied on point down in the alders with Dawn honoring her. I turned to Neb and said, "You're younger than I am—why don't you go down in those alders and pay tribute to those dogs by killing a bird for them?"

Fletcher and I stood on the point of the ridge we had all three been following, watching Neb honor Lady and Dawn. As we stood there, two grouse flushed wild from a small thicket some thirty feet in front of us and flew straight away, flying low and following the contour of the land, which fell away into a rather open valley. They then swung up to the left about a hundred yards, pitching into the woods on a ridge higher to our left.

You probably are wondering why Fletcher and I did

not shoot at those two grouse as they flew straight away in the open. We do not shoot wild flushed birds when hunting with our dogs (not even old dogs), because we love to watch the dogs handle grouse once they find them. The grouse is king of all the upland birds, and we hunt grouse for sport.

Neb had done his duty for Lady and Dawn by shooting an adult grouse that tried to escape Neb's quick action with his light 20 gauge and No. 8 shot. While Lady was retrieving the grouse, Dawn came running up in front of Fletcher and me. When she came into the vicinity from which the two grouse had flown, she threw her head high and ran directly down the flight line the birds had taken; then she disappeared into the cover on the ridge high on our left. Neb and Lady had joined us on the ridge, and Lady went on ahead, quartering the valley, then also fading into the cover near where Dawn had gone in. When we could see what was taking place, we found Dawn pointing towards a large popple windfall that apparently had fallen while the leaves were still green, for they were clinging to the limbs but had turned dark brown. Lady was there, too, backing Dawn. As we stood some yards from the dogs, Fletcher and I heard the voice of an honest-to-goodness grouse hunter. Neb said, "Let's gang up on these two birds and maybe we can get both of them. Fletcher, you go wide around to the right and a few yards forward. I'll go wide to the left and forward. Jack, since you own the dogs, you go in and flush the birds. If they fly straight ahead of you, shoot between Fletch and me, and Fletch and I can both shoot, if need be. If they fly between you and Fletcher, I can shoot between you two. If they fly between you and me, Fletcher can shoot between us." With everyone in position, I walked in and kicked the windfall. The bushy end of the tree exploded and out went both grouse straight ahead of me about four feet apart. I nearly erred by pulling on the left bird which was rightly Neberle's bird. As I was about to squeeze the trigger, the bird started falling. I eased the barrel of my Model 12 Winchester 20 with skeet tube to the right and touched off the trigger. The second grouse fell just a few feet beyond the first bird. The sound of our shots were one right on top of the other. The dogs retrieved the grouse and were heeled up, for we were not far from my car on this last super piece of dog work.

Neb is the stylish and methodical grouse hunter. When he sees his dog on point, he looks all around before flushing the bird and says to himself, "If I were a grouse, where would I go to depart and get out of sight as quickly as possible?" Most of the time, he guesses correctly as to where the bird will try to escape. Percentage-wise, this thinking usually makes the hunting more productive. Neb did say as we talked about his style later that day, "You know, Jack, that king of game birds still outsmarts me more often than I do him."

When we reached my car, Lady and Dawn were eager to get into the dog trailer for a well-deserved rest after a seven-hour hunt. We headed for the place Neb had chosen for a late afternoon hunt with Windy and Dusty, which was about a twenty-minute drive.

Neb's wife, Jane, who liked to watch the dogs work, was to meet us at an old wagon trail off the main road about four o'clock. She was waiting for us when we arrived at the turnoff into the trail which ran along on old fence surrounding an abandoned wooden house. We stopped about a hundred yards in on the trail. As we got out of the car, Neb said, "See that old leaning post over back of the house by the apple tree? For years I have stopped here, and every time I get out of the car, a grouse has always flushed from near that tree, and I have never had a dog work on him." He had no more than said it when a grouse bolted out from under the apple tree and into the heavy cover beyond. Windy and Dusty were turned loose on our left through some pin cherry trees and down towards the cedar swamp. The forest floor along the swamp was covered with wintergreen. Windy was on point there in a few minutes, with Dusty backing. The procedure here was routine, and Windy brought the dead bird in to his owner. Shortly, Dusty had a nice find with Windy backing. Both dogs combed the swamp edge and potholes on the side, and Windy came up with two more nice grouse finds right where Jane could observe the stylish dogs and men in their favorite sport.

Darkness comes a bit earlier along the cedar swamps than it does in the more open cherry ridges, and when Neb shot the last grouse Windy pointed that evening, you could see the fire belch from the end of his gun barrel. All three of us were in our mid-thirties, and an all-day grouse hunt was just another enjoyable day behind us.

This day was pleasantly different from many other hunts because we were all invited to have dinner at the home of Mrs. Carscallen, Fletcher's mother, on Rifle River near Selkirk, Michigan. Hunters are always hungry after a long day in the Michigan woods, and this dinner hour was no exception. Mrs. Carscallen smiled as she enjoyed our chatter about the day's hunt and about her most delicious meal.

After all the thanks and goodbyes, I boarded my old Buick and headed for the Ogemaw Hills Hotel in West Branch, just a few miles away, where I would be staying during a ten-day grouse and woodcock hunting trip. I sometimes had a bad habit of falling off to sleep while driving; so in order to keep from doing this I often would sing as I drove along. Since I was a bit weary, this seemed to be the time for me to sing. The Buick purred like a kitten as we rolled along in the cool evening dampness, and I sang that old song, "The End of a Perfect Day." The song is beautiful, but I'm not sure the singing was all that good. I can't whistle either, but I did stay awake.

Slab Town

In the 1870s the little town of Farwell, Michigan, expanded with the lumbering of the virgin white pine of the area. Sawmills sprang up near the town's border and soon extended several miles to the west and south. The one good sawmill that boasted a circular saw was located at the southwest edge of Farwell, and huge piles of slab wood surrounded the outlying mills. The families who lived and worked along the lumber trails used the wood for their heating and cooking; hence the name, Slab Town.

Following the lumbering days, some folks in the area took up small farming, but, after a few years, they gradually left until all of them had moved away. There are some tell-tale basements where part of the stone foundations are still visible. Near these there are a few apple trees that have long been neglected, along with lilac bushes that have become stunted or scrubby because the inhabitants and dwellings have long been gone. The white pine stumps—the tell-tale marks of the proud and majestic white pine of a century ago—are still there, like quiet ghosts within the rich, dense wilderness. With the exception of approximately three hundred acres out of nearly six square miles, Slab Town has reverted to the state of Michigan.

When I came to this area with my family in 1943, one could move from thirty to fifty grouse in a three-hour afternoon hunt. While this has not been the case in the past few years, Slab Town is still a great place to work a good grouse dog.

Another grouse find in the Slab Town area. Note the bell on this Setter.

Know Something Special About Your Dog

It would be wise to keep in mind something special about your dog, whether it be a physical marking or something unusual that he does, should it ever become necessary for you to have to identify him to a stranger who has found your dog when he is lost or hurt.

As an example, in the fall of 1981, a friend from Pennsylvania was running his dog in a grouse trial in Michigan. When the dog did not show up at the end of the course he was running on and was not found that night, my friend alerted all the people at the trial to be on the lookout for his dog Beau. The trials lasted nearly twelve days. Nothing was heard about the dog. My friend notified the conservation department, the state police, the sheriff's office, and the newspaper before he left for his home in Pennsylvania.

Someone had picked up the dog while it was competing in the trial. His collar had a brass nameplate with my friend's name, address, and phone number. The person who actually stole the dog disposed of the collar he was wearing, replaced it with a nylon collar (no nameplate), put a small dog bell on the dog, and apparently took him grouse hunting. The dog must have run away from the thief, because one month after the grouse trial, I received a phone call from my friend in Pennsylvania, who said that the Humane Society in Harrison, Michigan, had contacted him and told him that he could come and identify the dog. Because it was a long trip from Pennsylvania and could prove to be fruitless, he asked me if I would go there to identify the dog and then call him with the results.

I went to the Humane Society in Harrison to identify this Setter dog. In good condition, he weighed sixty pounds plus. He was now very thin, down to a little over forty pounds, but the Society had cared for him well. I had known this dog since he was a puppy, besides having seen him run in many trials, but it was difficult for me to be positive that he was actually my friend's Setter dog Beau. When I called my friend to tell him that, he said, "I don't want to drive all the way to Michigan if you're not sure it's Beau." I then asked him if Beau had any special markings I could look for, and my friend could not remember any.

"Does the dog do something special that only you know he can or will do?" I asked.

"Yes," he said, "Get a pan of dog food, take him to a spot by himself, hold the pan up high and ask him to say 'please,' and he will bark twice.

Going back in the kennel room, I got a pan of food and let the dog out of his kennel. Holding the pan of food up, I said, "Say 'please.'" The dog stood up on his hind feet, danced around for about twenty seconds, then barked twice.

While this was going on, my friend was holding on the phone. I told him the good news, saying that the dog didn't bark very loudly, but he did bark twice. My friend replied, "That's him, that's Beau. I'll come and get him."

So it does pay to be aware of those special things about your dog.

Rippi of Webster Woodlands, a male Vizsla.

You Be the Judge

Do bird dogs think? I once read that the extent of a dog's thinking ability is very limited. Maybe, but I believe it depends on his intelligence. Some dogs are smarter than others and seem to have an advantage over the dogs with lesser intelligence.

Many years ago, I had a classy little Setter by the name of King's Chief General, called Windy. He was an All-Age and ran and hunted like one every time that he was put down.

Windy was the type of dog that stayed around the yard and could be trusted in the house anytime during the day but spent nights in his kennel and made no fuss about it. He seemed to accept things in stride. My wife often let Windy in the house during the day, and he would take up his favorite spot in a corner.

Most often when I would come home in the evening, my boots came off and my bedroom slippers would take their place. Windy would watch me get my slippers, and one night, when I was sitting in the big chair taking off my field boots, he got up from his little corner, went through the bathroom to the bedroom, and brought me one of my slippers, then quickly went out again and brought the other one. No one had taught Windy to do this.

My foster mother had belonged to the Alpha Chi Omega sorority while going to college, and the sorority's whistle was used around our home any time one of us was needed. When I married Ruth Gordon in 1928, she, too, was an Alpha Chi Omega, and we also used the Alpha Chi whistle whenever we wished to call one another around our kennel place.

One evening Windy was lying under the big elm tree near the house. Not realizing that Windy paid attention when Ruth and I would signal each other with the Alpha Chi whistle, Ruth whistled for me to come when supper was ready. Immediately, Windy came running to the kennel where I was doing some work. When Windy reached the screen door at the kennel, he barked at me, then started back to the house. When I did not come, he returned to the kennel door and barked more vigorously. I went to the door and he headed towards the house, but hesitated until I came with him. When I arrived at the house, Ruth told me what Windy had done when she had whistled for me. After that evening, whenever Ruth would whistle for me while Windy was around loose in the yard, he would come running to where I was, look at me with pleading eyes, and then take me to the house.

I had another dog named Windy's Pride. He, too, was called Windy and was the grandsire of the one in the above story. I will refer to him as Pride. He was very intelligent and did many outstanding things that caused me to wonder about a dog's intelligence.

I loved to spot hunt for grouse. When the thorn apples were ready and the grouse were having feasts on them, I would put Pride in the seat of my pickup and drive from one thorn apple thicket to another. Pride would sit up in the seat watching eagerly for each and every thorn apple thicket. Grouse hunters know that hunting alone in thorn apples is rather tricky, but with Pride, a beautiful, blue belton Setter, it was sheer magic and very productive for the two of us. When I would let Pride out of the truck near the thorn apples, he would move swiftly but quietly, ghost-like, towards the thicket. If grouse were there, he would point and wait staunchly until I would get a few yards from his stand; then he would back off slowly and run around quickly and quietly to the other end of the thicket and make a staunch hard point. That would be when the explosion would occur at my end of the thicket. The field day was on as the grouse bolted out near me. With Pride, I did not need a shooting partner to cover the other end. In sixty-two years of grouse hunting and more than that number of good dogs, I had no other dog that made this smart maneuver.

In an article I once read in a sporting magazine, the author spoke of a dog's thinking capabilities. He gave an example of what would happen if, during a hunt, a dog came to a log or footwalk over a ditch or stream. The dog's action would be similar to that of a horse in this instance. The horse would prefer to make his way through the water unless he was led over the bridge by someone. During a hunt, a dog will almost always negotiate the stream itself rather than a log or a bridge.

In my opinion, good, intelligent bird dogs do think.

Fred Leggett's Setter Dog Pete

In his later years Fred Leggett, who is now deceased, retired to his cottage near the Au Gres River and the village of McIvor, Michigan, to write occasional articles about field trials and bird dogs.

On a small slope near Fred's cottage was a kennel building with an outside run that sloped towards a small trout stream. That was where Fred's Setter dog Pete made his home. Pete had an open box-type bed inside the shelter building just above the entrance so he could go in and out at will. However, Pete developed a habit of going out into the run in the night and barking loudly and continually. This annoyed Fred even though he had no close neighbors. A drop door was put on the entrance to the shelter so that Pete was shut inside at night. Fred hoped this would stop the nocturnal barking. It worked only for a few nights and then Pete began barking again and barked even more than before.

Fred's night garments consisted of a stocking-style nightcap with a tassel, and a long, flannel nightshirt. The dog's barking irritated Fred to the point where he would don his slippers, go out in his nightcap and nightshirt, and whack the side of Pete's shelter with a shovel or broom, telling Pete to be quiet. This quieted Pete only long enough for Fred to get snugly into bed.

The disturbance went on for a few nights, and Fred's patience was worn to a frazzle. The next day, Fred bored a hole through the dog-shelter wall just above Pete's box bed. A long coil of rope was readied outside the lower end of the kennel-run fence a few feet from the trout stream. That night, when it came time to shut Pete inside the shelter for the night, Fred ran the coil of rope through the end of the kennel-run fence, through the hole in the shelter wall, and fastened it to Pete's collar. Several feet of rope were left outside of the kennel fence where Fred could get hold of it if need be.

About midnight, when Fred was sleeping, Pete went on a noisy barking spree that aroused Fred. Sliding into his slippers, he went out in his nightcap and flannel nightshirt. Fred, being a tolerant man, picked up the rope at the end of the kennel run and gave it a sharp jerk. Pete came up against the inside wall of the shelter with a thud and the barking ceased immediately.

Elated about his accomplishment, Fred strolled back to his cottage and to bed. Lo and behold, about 2:30 in the morning, Pete took off on another barking spree, worse than before. This raised a very angry Fred straight up in bed. He ran down to the kennel again in his night clothes and picked up the end of the rope at the end of the kennel run; holding tightly to the rope, he ran down the slope towards the trout stream as fast as he could run.

You guessed it. Pete had chewed the rope loose from his collar, and Fred ended up in that ice-cold, trout stream water up to his armpits. Maybe dogs do think!

What Is a Good Grouse Dog?

Grouse dogs differ greatly in the way they handle a bird because of the very nature of the bird. First, the bird lives in a wooded area that has much bottom cover. Mr. Grouse is forever alert to the odd noises and unusual movements of objects in his habitat; the percentages are in his favor.

Without a doubt there are as many different methods of working grouse used by bird dogs as there are methods used by various owners. For example, an old-timer told me one day, "Always wear wool stag pants, never these new-fangled, briar-proof pants or chaps—they're too noisy." Some people like a slow, plodding-type dog that points and walks in a pointing manner when following a grouse. Another dog may ground-trail a grouse for several hundred feet before the grouse stops long enough for the dog to point, with his owner walking along following the dog so that he will be in shooting range when the grouse takes to the air.

Some bird dogs make game; i.e., they do not stop and point. They indicate to the owner by their actions that there is or has been a grouse near, then go moving around to get closer to the bird. In most cases, the grouse of today will not tolerate these actions but will flush wild. Sometimes this type of dog causes the grouse to fly up into a tree and sit. The dog owners themselves are as variable in their hunting methods as their dogs.

A method productive for one owner might not be so for another. If the methods both the man and his dog use are productive to putting grouse in the game bag, that's really what counts.

Today's grouse dog must first possess an acute nose. His running gait should be such that, when he gets scent of a grouse, he can stop immediately, and, of course, stay there. Once he has pointed, he had better not try to make game by moving around to a better scenting position, because, if he does, more than likely the bird will flush on him.

Naturally, the weather and scenting conditions always play a major role in how the dog can handle the bird. Strong winds make it extremely difficult for even a good, wise bird dog to handle grouse, because the birds are very wary on windy days—more so than on still days. Once the dog resorts to dropping his head and working ground scent, he has "lost the ball," so to speak. Also, as I mentioned earlier, I watch the dog's gait. I do not consider a "brush buster," for such a dog is sometimes mistaken for a dog with drive. My type of grouse dog must run, and his speed should match his nose, not exceed it. His ghost-like manner of running is essential to his ever developing into a good grouse-handling dog. You cannot expect a dog to become a good grouse dog if he goes through the woods sounding like a bull in a china shop. A good grouse dog, besides having natural abilities, should check on his hunter frequently, unless he is on point.

Tobacco River Crockett, pointing grouse in Slab Town, December 1980. Photo by Jane Jaime.

A Dog's First Grouse-Hunting Season

It is normal for a young bird dog to go hunting when let out of a car carrier, even though he has had a course in yard work. For seasoned hunters with a young, first-season bird dog, there are things to remember. First, the dog is not going to act or respond in the same manner as your old dog did at eight to ten years of age. The young dog is very likely going to be eager to get started. When the hunter arrives at the place he wishes to start grouse hunting, he should be completely ready himself; that is, have his boots on, and have all of his gear, his shotgun, and his shells all ready to go before he turns the dog loose to go hunting.

The system is simple. The hunter and the dog hunt together, not each by himself as could happen if the dog is turned out of the carrier before the hunter is ready to start. After the dog has a season or two using this system, he will settle down, knowing that he and his hunter are a team working together.

If the hunter expects the dog to handle in the woods, he should not follow the dog. A course or direction should be chosen so that the dog will learn to check on his hunter periodically. If the hunter follows the dog, two things, besides the dog not handling, can happen in the grouse woods: First, the dog will have the hunter following him all of his life while hunting; second, a dangerous habit may develop. For example, the hunter may choose to hunt an expansive new area. By following the dog, both could get lost and spend hours trying to locate the place where the hunt started.

Through the years, I have taught or encouraged amateurs who are hunting the young dog during his first season on grouse and woodcock, never to shoot a wild flushed bird, or a bird that the dog has not pointed. This final practice is most important. Some hunters are a bit quick on the trigger and have a habit of shooting every bird that flushes in gun range, especially a wild flushed bird or a bird the dog has knocked or routed into flight, whether the dog is involved or not.

Do the following, for the first and perhaps the second grouse hunting season. Carry your shotgun, unloaded, over your arm. Have shells handy so that when your young dog points and holds, you can drop a shell or two into your gun as you approach the dog. Make every effort to kill the bird so your dog can retrieve it if he is so inclined. It is as simple as one, two, three.

1. *Do not* shoot wild flushed birds.
2. *Do not* shoot birds that the dog flushes.
3. *Only* shoot birds when the dog is staunch on point.

The more intelligent your dog is, the quicker he realizes his reward comes only after you shoot the birds he points and holds.

It does not matter what type of shotgun you use, whether it is an autoloader, side by side double barrel, over and under, or pump gun. I shoot most often my Winchester Model 12-20 gauge with polychoke, but I have a side by side Ithaca Model 100 grouse gun with single trigger, twenty-five-inch barrels, bored cylinder and improved cylinder. This is a nice brush gun, which I carry broken over my arm while hunting so that when my young dog points I can drop a shell or two into the chamber as I approach the dog. With auto loaders and pump guns, a shell or two can be carried in the magazine, with the breech open. As you approach your young dog on point, pump or load a shell into the chamber. This system makes good grouse and woodcock dogs.

Try it.

What Is a Blinker?

A blinker is a dog that points, but, as his handler approaches, leaves his pointing position, going off to hunt as though there were no bird where he had pointed. The dog will do this every time the handler gets near him while pointing. This habit usually is caused by too-harsh treatment by the handler while the dog is closely associated with a bird, generally when the dog has knocked a bird, with the result that the dog becomes afraid of the handler. Blinking is a difficult habit to overcome or cure. If the handler/owner realizes the mistake he has made and likes the dog well enough, he can rebuild the dog's confidence by starting from scratch. By that I mean let the dog become entirely unbroken and chase birds as if he were a puppy. This is not always the easiest thing to do, which brings me to a Setter dog named Kenru Sam, owned by a neighbor, Ken McLaughlin. Sam was a litter brother to Tobacco River Bill and Spartan Sage. He was class personified. He placed in trials as a puppy and developed into a good-looking Derby prospect. There were high hopes for Sam as time for the Grouse Futurity approached in the fall of 1962.

One day late in August, some friends, who owned the sire of Sam, called and wanted Ken and me to bring Sam and my dog Bill to their kennel so that they could shoot some pigeons over the dogs. So, Ken and I took the dogs to our friends' place. It was decided that we would put two pigeons in a Stuart Game Bird Releaser hidden in a weed patch near the kennel, and that one of our friends, Dr. H. E. Beckmeyer, would shoot the birds when flushed. The area where the birds were hidden was small and surrounded by tall trees. Sam was turned loose. He quickly found and pointed the birds in the Releaser.

Up to this time, Sam had pointed many birds, and had been shot over with a blank pistol and .410 shotgun many times, accepting training naturally during the process. As I flushed the birds in front of Sam, the loaded shotguns were emptied in rapid fire, but no birds were killed. Sam turned tail, ran off to the corner of the fence, and lay there shaking, scared to death.

On the way home Ken and I discussed Sam's future. I decided to go along with Sam by starting from scratch, with only seven weeks before the Grouse Futurity. Wearing an old army fatigue coat with large pockets, I put two pigeons in each pocket and took Sam to my training field. I turned Sam loose, letting him run. When he came near me, I released a pigeon from my pocket. The first time the dog saw the flying pigeon, he turned and ran the other way. I could see that this was adding injury to misery. I put a twenty-five foot check cord on Sam and let him run, dragging the check cord. As he would come near, I'd catch the check cord, release a pigeon from my pocket, then take off chasing the pigeon myself, at the same time saying, "Come on, Sam, let's catch him." This took some doing because, at first, Sam was reluctant to join in the chase. I went through this procedure twice a day for two weeks before Sam decided to join me in the chase. Of course, no shots were fired during these sessions. The third week I decided again to release a pigeon from my pocket when Sam was running along close to me dragging his check cord. Letting the pigeons go I said, "Catch him, Sam," and he chased that pigeon at least one hundred yards. This encouraged me. The next week, after Sam had chased at least forty birds by himself, I hid two pigeons in Releasers about three hundred feet apart and worked Sam into the wind towards the hidden birds. Believe me, I was concerned as to whether Sam would point or not. Because of this, I also had two pigeons in my pocket. Sam pointed the first bird, but lacked intensity. As I approached, Sam backed off from the bird a few feet. I immediately let the pigeon go from my pocket, flushing the one from the Releaser simultaneously.

I worked the dog the opposite way from the second bird in the Releaser for about ten minutes before heading towards the second hidden bird. Sam had a nice breeze in his favor. He pointed the bird with intensity and style at a distance of forty feet. He stood for a few minutes, though he appeared ready to go whenever the bird flushed. This was an all-white pigeon. When the bird flushed, Sam chased it hard. When the dog and bird were about two hundred feet along a fence row, I shot the .22 blank (extra loud) pistol. It was a happy day, to see Sam continue chasing at the shot.

This procedure was continued two or three times daily for over a week. It was now the middle of October. Ken McLaughlin was concerned enough with Sam that he came by nearly every day to ask, "Are we going to the Grouse Futurity?"

"I'm not sure yet," I told him. "You know, if we go, we will have to leave here next Tuesday night."

The following Monday I decided to make sure that my efforts with Sam would not backfire on me. Going into the woods behind our kennel without the dog, I dizzied two pigeons, hiding them a couple hundred feet apart, one on the right of the path, the other ahead and on the left. I brought Sam and my .38-caliber blank pistol and turned Sam loose right back of the kennel. He quickly found the bird on the right, pointed staunchly and beautifully, letting me go kick the pigeon out from under a small pine tree. I shot the .38 immediately over the dog. He chased far along the swamp and came back when I called. He found the second bird and repeated his performance, even better because the bird was a bit too dizzy to take off. Sam stood well through this event and chased as I shot the .38 again. I heeled Sam up. My anxiety was relieved as we walked back to the kennel.

Just as Sam and I came to the rear of the kennel, there stood Ken McLaughlin. Again he asked, "Are we going to the Grouse Futurity?"

Enthusiastically, I told him, "Pack your bag. We leave tomorrow evening."

It was a long trip to Norwich, New York, with Sam and his brother Bill but it was well worth it, for Kenru Sam won the 1962 Grouse Futurity at Pharsalia, New York.

The trip home seemed much shorter, and we re-ran the trial several times as we drove down the highway.

So a blinker sometimes can be cured.

Kenru Sam, winner of the 1962 Grand National Grouse Futurity.

The Stuart Game Bird Releaser

It has occurred to me that readers might be interested in the why-and-how of the Stuart Game Bird Releaser, and the feasibility of the device.

It all started years ago; in 1949, to be exact. In and around the vicinity of our kennel in north central Michigan, the wild birds (grouse, woodcock, and pheasants) were few in number. Therefore, it was necessary to resort to liberated and controlled birds, which consisted mostly of common pigeons at that time, since pen-raised quail were not available as they are at present. At first, I used dizzy pigeons, which presented several problems. Either the bird would be awake and gone by the time the dog came into the area, or the bird would be too dizzy and would not take wing, which was a serious temptation to young dogs.

Next, I used a two-sided wire cage with a long string attached. All this really did was keep the bird where I put it until I got in the area with the dog. Again, when the dog pointed and the string was pulled, letting the two sides drop down, the bird did not always fly but sometimes just walked off, so only one thing was gained. The cage could only be called a bird holder. To be frank, I lay awake nights trying to figure a way to make a device that would actually catapult a bird into the air in full flight. One night, in 1950, I thought of a possible way this could be done. When I got up it was after 2:00 in the morning, and I drew a sketch of the idea on a piece of paper, then went back to bed. The idea kept "bugging me," and a little while later I got up again to make more concrete plans.

I worked nights in my basement workshop and built the first Releaser that would catapult a bird into the air five or six feet. Originally, my idea was intended for my own personal use, and my first Releasers were manually operated in various ways to try to make the results as natural as possible. Various people and customers who came to my place saw me using these manual devices while working the dogs and wanted one or two. In some cases, they insisted on the very ones I was using.

One day in 1951 the late John M. Hadaway, "Mr. Grouse," was at my place watching me work dogs with this device. He said, "You better get that patented." A couple of weeks later another good friend, Walter Bublitz, had me come to Bay City, Michigan, where he had made an appointment for me to bring my device to a patent attorney. A name for the device had to be decided upon; so, on the spot, "The Stuart Game Bird Releaser" was born. The manual Releaser was advertised in *The American Field* for many years, and frequently in *Field & Stream* as well as *Sports Afield*. In fact, the late Henry P. Davis wrote many articles about the Releaser, which were published in his dog column in *Sports Afield*, besides an illustrated feature article on the Releaser.

There were nearly fifty thousand manual Stuart Game Bird Releasers sold from 1952 to 1962, and during this period, I spent much time with various electronic engineers trying to develop a radio-controlled Releaser. If a controlled bird could be made to react like a wild bird, the dog would learn to respect it as he would a wild bird. About eight years were spent developing various electronic releasers, which presented problems at times. For example, such things as electronic fence controllers, airplanes and police-car radios, or electric high lines would set off the Releaser, flushing the bird prematurely.

One time I transported the birds to a birdy place in a field where I had previously placed two electronic releasers of the early style. After placing the birds in the releasers and covering them lightly with natural grasses, I went back to my car. Upon turning the key to start it, the surge from the coil by the motor triggered the releasers, tossing the birds into the air in full flight.

Sure, I had days when I would go right up the wall and want to give up the whole idea! Being of a determined nature, though, I kept at it until, in the late sixties, I perfected a model that functioned satisfactorily at least ninety-five percent of the time—the birds could be flushed by the handlers with their transmitters from zero to four hundred feet. The company then making the Stuart Game Bird Releasers found itself deep in contracts with the Navy, and in 1974, I began corresponding with Jerry Gonda of Tri-Tronics, Inc., in Tucson, Arizona, about manufacturing the Releaser.

Early in 1975 Jerry and I came to terms, and Tri-Tronics is manufacturing the finest Electronic Game Bird Releaser ever designed. The electronic equipment functions as near to one hundred percent of the time as possible. The Stuart Game Bird Releaser's original design, which had not been changed, had both sides open so that the air current passed under the bird and out the opposite side along the ground level. The air current passing over the bird would rise, striking the inside of the sloping doors and going upward into the higher level, thus causing the bird scent to permeate the area in and around the hidden bird from every possible angle. In short, the flow of the air current is upward, and out and

This photo was taken in 1950 and shows how the Stuart Game Bird Releaser catapults the bird into the air. It appeared in a feature article written by the late Henry P. Davis, in the September 1960 issue of *Sports Afield,* and in a later article by Bill Stetson in *Field and Stream.*

along the ground until it is dissipated. Naturally, the strength of the breeze or wind controls the distance of the dissipation. In addition, the overall dimensions are the same as the original ones—small and compact as possible, yet roomy enough so that the bird can move a little, thus emitting more scent. Also, the color factor of the Releaser has been taken into consideration. It is a neutral color so that it can be camouflaged easily with nearby grasses and weeds. The device has been developed through many years of experience. It is the best there is, and the best is none too good for a good bird dog.

Tri-Tronics is using better materials, such as an anodized aluminum body instead of wood, new-type adjustable spring-activated doors, and a new-style, comfortable springboard that holds the bird or birds in a natural, comfortable position until the Releaser is triggered by the handler with his transmitter. A pigeon can be catapulted six to nine feet in full flight, and quail (one or two birds) nine to twelve feet. A newly designed, unbreakable steel trigger assembly has been added, replacing the old-style cast-iron assembly.

In 1980 the Releaser was further improved with more power in the receiver so as to eliminate all possibilities of malfunction.

The chapter entitled "Training Pointing Dogs with the Electronic Game Bird Releaser" covers all phases of training pointing breeds, starting with the puppy and going on to the completely finished bird dog.

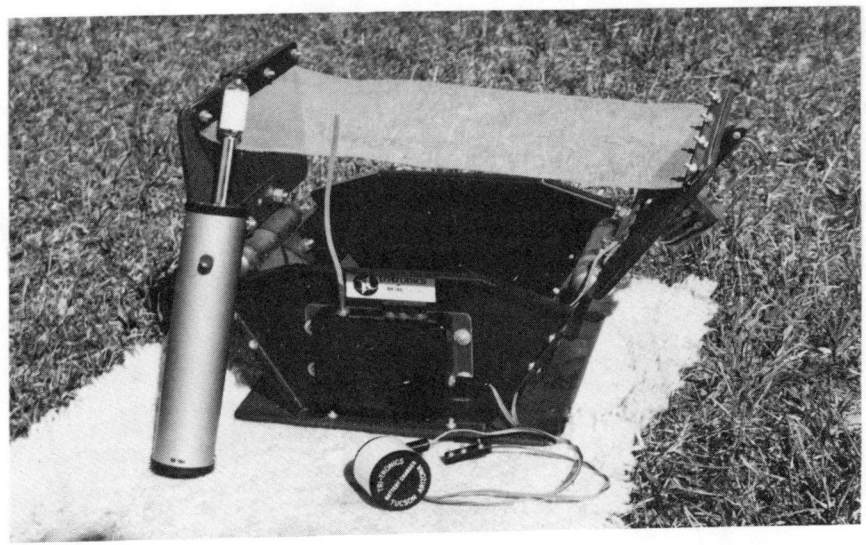

The Electronic Bird Releaser by Tri-Tronics, Inc. The releaser is in the open position, with hand transmitter and charger.

The Electronic Bird Releaser by Tri-Tronics, Inc., in the closed position.

Training Pointing Dogs with the Electronic Game Bird Releaser

It is very important to hide the Releaser in a birdy place, well concealed or camouflaged with natural grasses or weeds. When searching for birds, the dog can only detect the scent of the bird, not see the Releaser. Because there is no foot or ground scent, the puppy will learn to find and locate the bird with head high. This is especially advantageous for grouse dogs, since grouse will not tolerate a dog hustling on ground scent. The dog that points with head high is known as a "winder." The ground-working dog is known as a "trailer." Most class grouse and woodcock dogs are winders. The Electronic Game Bird Releaser develops high-headed winders.

By using the Releaser, you can start a puppy to hunt for the bird very naturally. How the best results are accomplished in all phases of training is strictly up to the handler/trainer with his hand- or pocket-held control transmitter. The procedure is simple. Working the puppy, hold the transmitter in your hand with your thumb ready to press the button instantly. The puppy may indicate he scents the bird, but not stop—he may go right on in. Without a Releaser, the bird, if it were wild, would flush. The instant you see the puppy turn towards the bird in the Releaser without stopping, you must press the button, releasing the bird into the air in full flight so that the puppy will give chase. This is the same reaction the puppy shows with a wild or native bird. This also is the time to introduce the puppy to the gun. While he is first chasing the bird vigorously, let the puppy go some distance, then shoot a .22-caliber blank pistol. After shooting several times while the puppy is quite far away, you can start shooting when the puppy is closer. By this time the puppy will have associated the report of the gun with the bird. In over fifty years, using the above method, this training kennel has never had a gun-shy puppy or dog.

After chasing the bird a few times, the puppy will no doubt establish a point. With your thumb ready to press the control button, walk slowly towards the pointing puppy and say absolutely nothing. When and if the puppy breaks to go in and flush, press the control button immediately. Follow this procedure every time the puppy is worked on birds. Sooner or later, depending on the puppy, he will stand until you reach him. Once the puppy can be handled, stroke him gently to build his confidence and make him staunch on point.

Assuming the puppy is far enough along in his training—and is also older— and has had yard training, you can work him with a check cord in two ways. If the young dog will stay on point until you reach him, you can then attach the check cord to his collar. If the bird is in a wooded area, you can pull the check cord taut around a tree close behind the dog, hold tightly to the end and do not jerk the cord, just keep it snug while returning to walk in front of the dog. When you near the bird-loaded Releaser, kick around in the ground cover a couple of times; at the same time, watch the dog. If he holds steady on point, press the control button, thus flushing the bird. Now, with the use of the check cord, you can start discouraging the dog from chasing the bird. Next you can teach the dog to stand to shot if you have not done so while teaching advanced yard training.

The same procedures can be used in open fields. However, you can choose to let the dog hunt with the check cord already attached to his collar, so that when he establishes a solid point, you can pick up the end of the check cord as you approach the dog to handle him on point. Stroke him gently; try to push him in on the bird. If the dog stiffens and pushes back, he is, in a sense, telling you that he doesn't want to flush the bird and is now ready to accept further training.

By this time the dog will be in his second season of training, or from eighteen to twenty-six months of age. Again, this varies from one dog to another. It pays to study your dog thoroughly at this stage of training, even though he still wants to chase the bird. Do not shoot over him any more while he is chasing. Catch him as soon as you can, bring him back to where he pointed, then shoot over him with the blank pistol. Do it every time, for this, besides making him steady to the gun, helps in breaking the dog completely from chasing the bird. Once he has learned to be steady to the shot, he will learn to wait on point, even though the bird has been flushed, until he is shot over.

In other chapters there are illustrations and clarifications of the procedures to be used in correcting your dog for chasing birds and breaking at the shot. The same methods or systems of correction are used when breaking dogs with a live bird in an Electronic Game Bird Releaser.

You can also teach the dog to back or honor another dog on point. If you work alone and have only one dog in training, teaching him to back presents a problem. However, a reasonable facsimile of a pointing dog can be made inexpensively of plywood, with iron stakes fastened to one front leg and one hind leg and extending eight or ten inches below the foot, so that the stakes can be pushed into the ground to hold the dummy pointing dog in position.

Make a setup without having your real dog around.

Jack Nicholson, assisting in a training session, going to hide an Electronic Releaser in a birdy place.

Completion of loading quail in the Electronic Releaser, just before the trigger is secured. Photo by Jack Nicholson.

Hide the Electronic Releaser in a birdy place, and always set the trigger assembly toward the wind direction. Photo by Jack Nicholson.

Final closing and latching of the Releaser. It is now ready to be hidden and covered lightly with surrounding grasses. Photo by Jack Nicholson.

Hold fingers of the left hand extended over the bird, while closing and latching the opposite door with the right hand. Photo by Jack Nicholson.

Camouflage the Releaser by covering it completely with surrounding grasses, leaves, or weeds. Make it look natural. Photo by Jack Nicholson.

The pointing instinct is bred right into the good dog. This one is seven weeks old.

Trainer checks to learn how staunch this young dog wants to be. Photo by Jack Nicholson.

The same puppy as pictured above, pointing a live bird in an Electronic Releaser at six months of age.

Once the trainer learns that the dog does not want to move in on the bird, he goes behind the dog and tries to push him in on the bird. This helps make the dog staunch. Photo by Jack Nicholson.

Card Shark pointing at twenty months of age. Photo by Jack Nicholson.

Teaching a young dog to back or honor his brace mate. Deke pointing a quail in an Electronic Releaser. Note helper with the transmitter, ready to flush the bird when the trainer shoots over the dogs.

Put a loaded Releaser in a birdy place. Downwind from the Releaser, place the plywood dog, pointing nicely twenty to thirty feet. Bring the real dog and work him for a few minutes before reaching the dummy pointing dog. Most dogs will back the dummy dog on sight; however, if the real dog is reluctant to back, it would be wise to bring him up behind the dummy dog on a check cord until he will back on sight voluntarily. Once he does, the rest is simple. You can stand alongside your backing dog, then press the control button, thus flushing the bird ahead of the dummy dog, and shoot the blank pistol.

If you have only the one dog, this system is astonishingly practical. It helps keep the real dog steady to wing and shot because the dummy dog positively will not chase the bird; besides, he is steady to shot, too.

Once the dog has been broken from chasing birds, it is not difficult to get him to stop to flush on a wild flushed bird. This is done with the Releaser by hiding it in cover but more or less in an open area on a day with a reasonable wind velocity. Work the dog towards the Releaser with the wind behind the dog. When he is within a reasonable distance, where it is certain that he will see the wild flushed bird (provided by you with the hand control), press the control button, thus flushing the bird. If the dog does not stop instantly (he should know the "whoa" term by this time), stop him, and bring him back to the spot where he should have stopped to flush. If he has already learned to stand to shot, you can shoot over him while he is standing; however, this is not compulsory. It is merely a matter of your choice. A bird dog can be taught all of the fundamentals pertaining to the complete training in conjunction with live birds, be they common pigeon, quail, small pheasants, or chukar partridge.

The inventor is the first to insist that the Releaser is a most valuable and successful training aid when used in conjunction with periodic workouts on native grouse, woodcock, quail, pheasants, or what have you!

If the dog presents a problem, or forgets his manners on a wild native bird, you can always remind him of his misdemeanor by using the Releaser once you return home. Do this as many times as needed to correct the problem.

The Electronic Game Bird Releaser is a valuable training aid. Naturally, to use the Releaser, it is necessary to have live birds, be they pigeons or quail. There are rather simple solutions to this need. If you live in a city or

The trainer placing the Electronic Releaser in the high grass in front of Sam, the plywood dog. Photo by Wally Brzenk.

Covering a loaded bird Releaser that is being set out in front of Sam. This setup is for teaching a bird dog to honor or back the pointing dog.

George, comfortably loaded in the Releaser. The Releaser is completely camouflaged with natural grasses. Photo by Wally Brzenk.

Magic Man and Tobacco River Crockett are turned loose, both voluntarily backing or honoring Sam on sight. The bird was flushed and can be seen between Sam and the trainer as it tops the hayfield.

small town, pigeons probably would not be the answer unless you live on or near the outskirts of the town. If this be the case, a box compartment with a small wired flight area can be attached to one end of a garage. The pigeons can be taught to come to that compartment from up to several miles from home. After the pigeons have lived in the compartment for a couple of weeks, let them out a few minutes just before dark or on a rainy day. They will fly around close and go back into their compartment through the upper opening with the one-way bobs. These gates, or pigeon traps, can be procured from Foy's Pigeon Supply, Box 27166, Golden Valley, Minnesota 55427. Foy's will send a catalog on request. For an illustration of the pigeon compartment, which will care easily for six to ten pigeons, see the following chapter.

Jim Owen, a friend who lived in Mishawaka, Indiana, had a Stuart Tri-Tronics Releaser. A farmer, who had a barn full of pigeons, gave him permission to train his dogs at the farm. Jim made a deal with the farmer's two boys, which involved calling them on the phone the day before he wanted to come to their farm and work his dog. The boys would catch a half-dozen pigeons, and Jim paid the boys fifty cents a bird. Occasionally, a bird would be shot for the dog, but most of the time the pigeons would return to the barn. This was an excellent arrangement because Jim did not have to house and feed his own pigeons; besides, it provided a place to work the dog. It also amounts to a good farmer-sportsman's relationship.

Quail are obtained quite easily since there are now many quail breeders. You can keep a dozen quail in town—even in the garage—in a cage where water and food are available for the birds. Then you can take the birds to the area where you want to work your dog. Attach a piece of strong, bright-red yarn securely to one leg of the quail, and load it in the Releaser—yarn and all—or the yarn can be strung on the outside of the Releaser. When the quail is flushed, watch where it lands. Do not work the dog on that bird, for it most likely will be tangled in the grass or weeds. The yarn helps you see where the quail has landed. You can locate the red yard, step on it, pick up your quail, and put it in your pocket to use again another day. If you wish to work the dog on quail more than once at the same training session, use another that has not already flown. Unless they are rested, pen-raised quail do not fly well or far if worked a second time the same day.

The trainer shoots a blank pistol over all three dogs as George goes to the loft. Photo by Jack Nicholson.

Tobacco River Crockett stops to flush as soon as George takes to the air. Photo by Wally Brzenk.

Magic Man knows how to stop to flush, too. The bird is on the horizon, straight ahead of the dog. Photo by Wally Brzenk.

Wally Brzenk, shooting the bird over Belle's nice stylish point.

Belle, hunting dead after the bird has been flushed and shot.

Belle was told to sit. The trainer then takes hold of her ear with his left hand, sticks his thumbnail into the top side of the ear, while saying "Give" and holding his right hand out to receive the bird. Photo by Wally Brzenk.

Belle finds the bird and starts back toward the trainer. Photo by Wally Brzenk.

The pigeon, home from field work with the dogs, on the landing board in front of the one-way trap. Photo by Wally Brzenk.

Belle is encouraged by the trainer to "Fetch" the bird directly to him. The check cord fastened to the trainer's belt is used when it is necessary to control the dog while hunting dead. Belle had already gone through that lesson. Photo by Wally Brzenk.

Attach a piece of red yarn, twenty-four to thirty inches long, on the leg of a quail, so that the bird can be found and used another time.

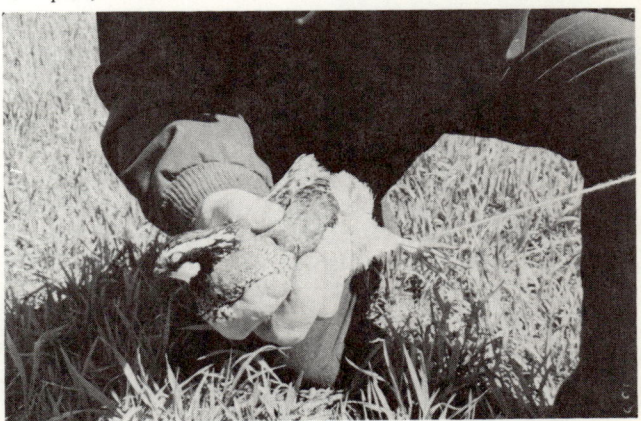

The Leader

It appears that there should always be a leader in whatever is to be accomplished. Our pigeon George has been just that at the Tobacco River Training Kennels for nineteen years. One never needs a net to catch George, for he is always ready to help work the dogs. He seems to sense when he is to tantalize and make a puppy "birdy" by flying low in circles, letting the puppy nearly catch up to him in his graceful flying maneuvers. However, he becomes more serious when older dogs, eager to learn, stand on point on the downwind side of the spot where George is resting comfortably in an Electronic Releaser. George seems to sense when the trainer/handler is close and lift-off is due.

As soon as the control button is pressed, he takes off quickly into the air, heading straight for his home loft. Once in the loft, George will go to the flight pen and sit on the cross pole. One only has to walk up to him and take him in hand, for he is always ready to entertain the dogs. Once placed in the Releaser, he will settle down as though resting. It appears that he enjoys his work.

There is no way one could guess how many dogs were started with George—learned to point, became staunch on point, steady to wing and shot, and learned to stop to flush and back another dog. George has no intentions of retiring from his daily work.

There goes George through the one-way trap. Photo by Wally Brzenk.

The author holding George, the nineteen-year-old wonder pigeon, before loading him into the Electronic Releaser. Photo by Wally Brzenk.

The Six- to Ten-Bird Pigeon Loft

The six- to ten-bird pigeon loft (also see illustration) should have the following features: (1) A clean-out feed-and-water drop door; (2) a one-way pigeon trap (the pigeon can enter from the outside, but cannot get out from the inside); (3) an outside flight cage (the cage frame is completely enclosed—bottom, top, and sides—with one-inch square-welded wire); (4) a bottom support frame of 1 by 2 feet (the balance of the inside frame can be either 2 by 2 feet, or 1 by 2—white pine is best); (5) an indoor bird compartment with the sides, top, and bottom made of 3/8-inch all-weather plywood; (6) an outside landing board, 1 by 12 by 36 inches, in front of a one-way trap on top of the wire flight pen. A landing board for the birds to walk into the one-way trap should be 1 by 10 by 12 inches long; (7) a two-way opening so the birds can go in or out of the flight pen. A hinged drop-door can be attached over the lower entrance, with hinges at the top of the cover and a screw eye near the bottom, and with a good cord attached to the screw eye.

To hold the cover open, run the cord up through the cage, pull the cord up, and then fasten it to a hook on the outside.

To chase pigeons out of the compartment into the flight pen, drop the lower cover down, and reach through the catch door at the end of the flight cage.

This miniature pigeon loft should be mounted low enough on a garage or outbuilding to allow easy access to food and water, yet high enough to keep stray dogs, cats, or other animals from annoying the pigeons. A cover of plywood or metal can be made to go over the one-way trap to keep cats, owls, or hawks from entering when the compartment is not in use, especially at night after the pigeons have gone to roost.

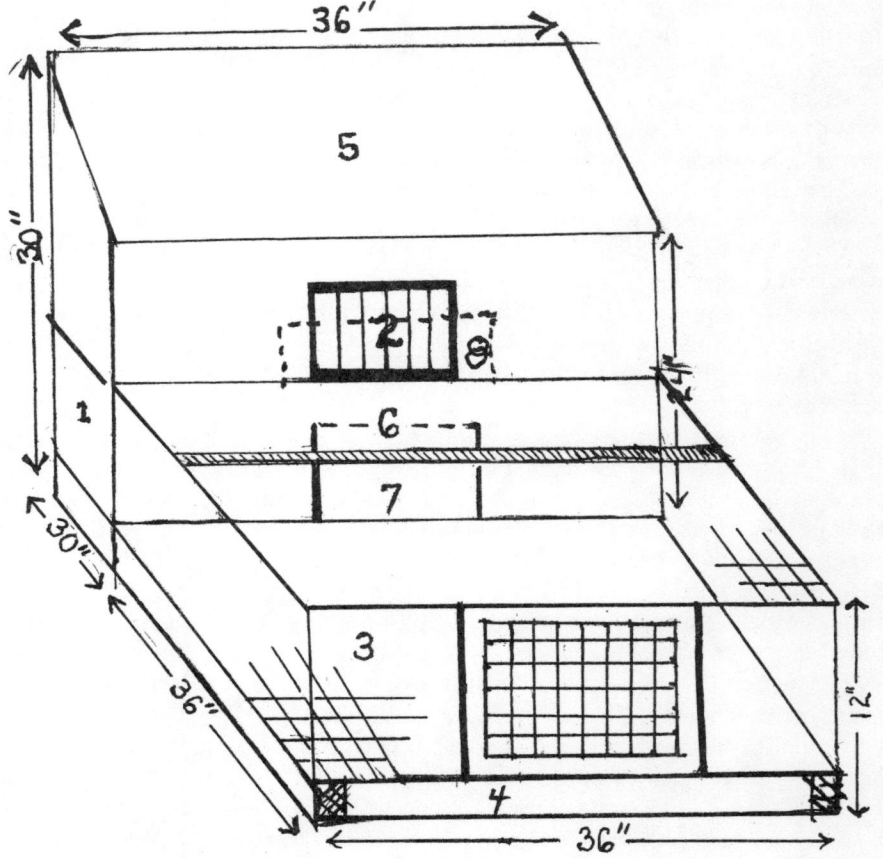

PIGEON LOFT
1. Drop door.
2. One-way pigeon trap.
3. Outside flight cage.
4. Bottom support frame.
5. Bird compartment.
6. Landing board.
7. Hinged drop door.

Training With Liberated Birds

Pen-raised quail are quite easily obtained. There are many game-bird farms that offer quail and other birds such as chukar partridge and pheasants. The bobwhite quail seems to be the most satisfactory for all-around training for bird dogs.

The recall cage, as shown in this chapter, should have a much larger protective cage over it with the sides and top covered with 2 by 4 inch welded wire. This keeps stray dogs, cats, racoons, and other animals from molesting the quail that are in the recall cage.

When releasing quail from the recall cage, *do not* set the cage down on the grass where you wish to release a couple of birds. Why? Because the dog will point where the cage sat on the grass. If you cannot hold the cage with one hand and release the birds at the same time, make a four-legged, portable frame to set the cage on while letting quail out of the recall cage.

To keep weasels, mink, or small possum from going in by way of the funnel of the recall cage, you should use wire mesh which is hinged flat on the outside of the reentry funnel, and which can be closed at night or whenever the cage is not being used.

A wheelbarrow is good, since you can leave the recall cage in the barrow and release the number of birds you wish in various places. Always manage to have from three to five birds in the recall cage when you return it to its original place. Later on in the day, the birds left in the recall cage will call the outside birds in. Always keep the feed and water containers inside of the recall cage.

It is not wise to work a dog that is not ready to stay on point at least long enough for you to regain personal control, because many times the quail will run or even expose itself—which is a serious temptation for a young dog. A check cord on the dog is necessary if you are to have control. It is best not to work a dog on liberated birds until he is staunch on point.

It is better to use a planted bird, be it quail or a common barn pigeon. This, of course, is only if the dog is old enough and has more or less graduated from chasing butterflies or song birds and has developed a desire for greater things—game birds.

Common barn pigeons have been used for many years by professional and amateur trainers. When resorting to the use of a barn pigeon, it is important that the bird be planted or hidden in a birdy place.

If using pigeons, tuck the bird's head under its wing, hold the bird in one hand, and swing it in a wide circle so that it will be dizzy; then hide it completely in cover by putting grass or weeds over it. Adding sticks or branches on top will cause the bird to stay put longer than if it is covered only with grass or weeds.

With this type of training, it is best to have a helper, especially if you choose to shoot the pigeon.

There is only one way you can work young dogs (six or seven months old) up to the stage where they want to point and hold. The way to do this is to put a pigeon in a strong old sock. Hide the pigeon in the sock and tie the top opening of the sock. Cover it with grass so that the dog cannot see it but can only smell it. Now, this is important—have a second pigeon in your pocket.

Work the puppy on a check cord into the wind towards where the pigeon in the sock is hidden. If the puppy points, fine. Try to handle him on point; while doing so, take out the bird that is in your pocket. Let it go directly in front of the puppy. He will, of course, chase, making him birdy. Immediately pick up the bird in the sock and put it in your pocket before the puppy has a chance to come back and catch it. When a dog of any age is in training, the more you can keep him from catching a bird the better.

A strong word of caution here: this type of bird work is sometimes exasperating for both man and dog. Try to keep the dog under control with the check cord. However, if the dog does happen to catch a bird, just take it away from him. Scold him, yes, but do not overdo punishment at this point because this is the time you must use common sense. Otherwise, the dog could become a "blinker."

This system can be used with pen-raised quail by dizzying the quail and working only a dog that will stay on point until you can reach him while he is standing.

If you work alone, the "trainer's helper" (see the chapter "Tools of the Trade") is an excellent device which can be made by anyone who does welding. If the dog still has a tendency to chase, a good piece of old shovel handle about six to eight inches long can be fastened to the end of the check cord in the following manner: With a three-cornered file or wood rasp, make a groove completely around the center of the handle and secure a piece of No. 9 gauge galvanized wire in the groove. Leave a wire ring large enough to fasten the end of the check cord. You do not have to wait until the dog is already on point before fastening the stick on the check cord because the cord will pass through the ring on the "trainer's helper" when needed.

When you approach the dog on point, you should

quietly attach the snap end of the cord to the dog's collar after running the cord through the ring on the "trainer's helper." You will control the dog while flushing the bird. Once the bird is flushed, if the dog chases it, you should drop the check cord. When the end of the cord with the piece of shovel handle attached reaches the ring in the "trainer's helper," it will stop the dog. It is important to watch this action closely. Just before the stick reaches the "trainer's helper," say only one word: "whoa." Also, do not shoot over the dog while he is chasing the bird. Rather, go and get the dog, say nothing, place his ear on the nameplate of his collar, and put thumbnail pressure on his ear as he is taken back to where he pointed. By all means, release the thumb pressure on his ear just before reaching the spot where he pointed. Once there, style him up, talk softly to him, then walk in front and shoot your blank pistol. If you wear an old hat or cap, throw it out front before shooting, make a noise like a flying bird, and then shoot. If the dog breaks, correct him again in the same manner. However, once the dog seems to lose interest, do not repeat this procedure until the next workout.

The above treatment is very effective and humane. Keep in mind, however, that a dog has two avenues of escape from training methods: (1) If you chastise the dog without controlling him by either having a firm grip on his collar or using a check cord, the dog can run off. (2) If the correction treatment is too severe, the dog will try to bite you. You should know absolutely when enough is enough.

A dog feels secure as long as he has four feet on the ground; therefore, there is another method you may wish to use rather than using pressure on his ear. Once the dog has been given the "whoa" order and stopped while chasing, go to him, get a good grip on his collar, pick him up high, and shake him vigorously while walking back with him to where he pointed. During this treatment, it is important to not say one word to him after the word "whoa." Once back to where he pointed, use the same method of praise as before.

A method similar to the preceding one is to get a firm grip on the dog's collar with your left hand, pick him up, reach over him, and grasp him in the right flank with your right hand, pinching him all the way back to where he pointed, then using the same type of praise as in the previous two methods.

Quail recall cage inside a guard cage, 5'x5'x30" high. Place near a large shade tree, when a woods edge is not available. This way the birds get some sun and shade each day.

Water container and feeder sitting on top of the recall cage. These are kept inside of the cage. Quail that are let out to work the dogs will return to the cage for feed and water. Photo by Wally Brzenk.

Close-up of a recall cage inside of the guard cage. The guard cage keeps out cats and stray dogs. Bird dogs being worked near the cage soon learn to stay away from the cage once they start finding quail out away from it.

Close-up of the recall cage, set up on 2 x 2's so that the droppings won't build up under the cage. Note the stick alongside the spot where the return funnel is located, helping the birds get back in the cage. Photo by Wally Brzenk.

Trainer wheels the recall cage full of quail into the field in a wheelbarrow to the spot where he wishes to release some quail prior to working the dogs.

Combination holding-and-recall quail pen, showing the guard fence around it to keep stray dogs from disturbing the birds.

Quail walks out of the cage onto the door, then either jumps on the ground and runs to the nearest weed patch, or flies a short distance and hides. Sure it's work, but it beats walking your legs off behind a good young prospect for an hour without finding any birds. Photo by Wally Brzenk.

Quail, entering the chute on the combination pen.

This system has worked successfully for the last twenty years at Tobacco River Kennels. Do not use a whip. It isn't necessary, and, what's more, you will have a much happier finished dog using Jack Stuart's humane system.

You should use several check cords of different lengths. The reason for this is that bird dogs are not as dumb as you might think. They learn how long the rope is. While working a dog, you can tell when the training starts taking effect because the dog will stop four or five feet short of the end of the cord or even before a trainer says "whoa." If you started with the 40- or 50-foot check cord, and the dog has learned about the length, go to a 25- or 30-foot check cord until the dog learns the length of the shorter cord. Go to a 10- or 15-foot cord and go through the same procedure with each different length check cord until you are down to a 4- or 5-foot cord. Be sure to use your choice of chastisement each time you correct him with the various lengths of cord.

You are probably wondering why you could not use one 40- or 50-foot cord and just take a shorter hold on it once the dog stops short of the end. You can, but the varied length check cords is a better way because, when the dog will stay on point without dragging a check cord, you should carry or drag the cord. Walk slowly to the pointing dog. Do not say anything such as "easy now," "steady," or "hold it." These remarks are superfluous and only tend to disturb the pointing dog. Once you reach the dog on point, you can go on one knee beside him, style him up by stroking him gently, and push him towards the bird, also gently but firmly. If he pushes back, he is telling you he does not want to disturb the bird, and he is asking to be broken.

Actions speak louder than words, so during the above process, say *absolutely nothing*. Just quietly fasten the necessary check cord to your dog's collar—and the rest has already been mentioned. By all means, do not keep saying "good boy" or "good girl" over and over while going through the procedure.

I know a couple of amateur trainers who "good boy" and "good girl" their dogs to death. What you *do* is what counts and is helpful to the dog, not what you say.

Remember to have top quality tools such as a very strong collar on the dog—one with an end dee ring is best since it has the double thickness of leather when stop pressure is applied to the dog. Have a check cord made of cotton; your hardware dealer can get it for you. Ask for sash cord three-eighths to one-half inch in diameter. A good-sized brass harness snap or barrel snap is good. These are good beginning tools. You will not find a whip of any kind in the chapter "Tools of the Trade."

The above system is the way to come up with a happy hunting dog and companion.

Cherokee, alert but steady as the bird is flushed in front of her.

Ollie, a son of Champion Ghost Train, learning not to creep or jump in and flush his birds after pointing. Handler approaches the dog from the rear and pushes the whoa stake into the ground behind the dog. The check cord has already been passed through the ring on top of the whoa stake. The dog is then styled up. Photo by Wally Brzenk.

Wally Brzenk shoots a common pigeon for this young Setter female.

The handler takes hold of the end of the check cord and walks in front of Ollie to flush the bird, keeping the check cord taut. Photo by Wally Brzenk.

The bird is flushed in front of Ollie, and the shot is fired while the dog is held in position with the check cord and the whoa stake. Photo by Wally Brzenk.

On the way back to the vehicle after a field workout on birds, the young dog gets advanced yard work on heeling when the trainer steps on the knotted stop check cord. Photo by Wally Brzenk.

Field Work

Depending on how well the puppy has accepted and progressed in his earlier yard work, you can now expose him to field work where he can search for wild birds or released or controlled birds, whichever may be obtainable. Once the dog points, a fifty-foot check cord can be used to advantage, since the dog has already become accustomed to it during his yard training.

When the dog stays on point, you can walk to him, handle the dog by stroking him gently, and style him up; that is, encourage the dog to keep his tail up. Push on his hindquarters on the hips. Pushing him towards the bird helps the dog to become intense and staunch on point, providing he pushes back, indicating he does not want to jump in and flush the bird. As I mentioned before, when he does this, he is asking to be broken in his own way.

Have control of the check cord. As in yard training, walk a few steps to the side before going in front of the dog to flush the bird. When the bird is flushed and the dog chases after the bird, hold tight to the check cord. Just before the dog reaches the end of the slack in the check cord, say "whoa." Bring the dog back to the spot where he pointed. Two rules of thumb: (1) Drop a red handkerchief where the dog pointed, for it is very important that the dog be brought back to the exact spot where he pointed. (2) Once the dog allows you to walk in front of him and flush the bird, he should be discouraged from chasing the bird.

Any chastisement should take place where the dog was stopped from chasing the bird. The word "chastise" means punish; however, the proper treatment at this point is most important. The training method that I have used most effectively is to take hold of the dog's collar once he is stopped, place his ear on the nameplate of his collar, and then press the ear with my thumbnail. The dog lets me know how much I can press on his ear. I do this all the way back to where he pointed. Just before reaching the pointing spot, I release the ear completely. The dog should never be chastised at the spot where he pointed. He should be praised.

This treatment should be repeated every time he chases the bird and until he remains on point. The dog eventually will understand that it is much better to stay in the pointing position.

When back at that spot, style him up again, stroke him gently, and praise him. Make him stand a few minutes.

Before sending the dog on, shoot the blank pistol. If he jumps at the shot, set him back. This procedure can be repeated as many times as necessary to have the dog stand to shot. All this, of course, if the dog has already associated the shot with the bird in his earlier training when he was allowed to chase.

Although for some years I trained bird dogs generally for all game birds, I have spent the past thirty-eight years training various breeds of pointing bird dogs as grouse dogs. The dogs are trained to hunt to the gun in the woodlands and are generally known as "cover dogs."

These dogs, during the early summer months, are put through all the formalities prescribed earlier, learning how to be comfortable, mannerly bird dogs.

Going to the grouse cover in early autumn, the training

The helper flushes the bird in front of Cherokee. She stands stylishly while watching the flight of the bird.

Tobacco River Billie, pointing a single quail during a field workout. A Derby dog learning the art of bird handling with style.

Showing a little affection and praise after a job well done by a good young Derby dog. Tobacco River Billie enjoys it.

Before sending the dog on, shoot the blank pistol over him.

Direct Route pointing a single quail with intensity and style.

A German Shorthaired Pointer, eleven months old, pointing.

continues with one exception: the trainer can carry two rubber balls on the adjustable cords and snap, which is called an Equalizer (see the chapter "Tools of the Trade"). You can carry the Equalizer easily on your belt. When the dog establishes a point, try to fasten it on the dog's collar. The rubber balls on the Equalizer should be adjusted to fit the dog so that he will step on the rubber balls when he runs. This action obviously will frustrate him, and he will slow down. It is also good to make your dog hunt close in the cover. The same procedure applies when working the dog on native grouse and woodcock, as when working the dog on controlled, planted, or liberated pen-raised birds, such as quail, chukars, or common pigeons.

Remember to use your yard training when getting ready to start the hunt and when going back to your vehicle at the end of the hunt. For example, use "whoa" before starting the dog to hunt and whenever needed during the hunt, and when heeling the dog back to the vehicle at the end of the hunt. If practiced every time, these procedures become automatic in the relationship between the master and his dog.

After a training session in the field, snap the stop cord on the dog and let him drag it. Tell him to heel, and if he tries to go ahead of you, say whoa, then step on the stop cord. He will soon learn to stay beside you when told to heel. Photo by Jack Nicholson.

Always heel your dog to the vehicle at the end of a training session. Photo by Jack Nicholson.

Jo's Aversion to Woodcock

Early one morning in the fall of 1936, Alex Adams, from Port Huron, Michigan, and I stopped for breakfast at a log cabin restaurant near Lincoln, Michigan.

There appeared to be very good grouse cover across the road from this place. We asked the owner if he knew who owned the land across the road. "I do," he replied. Asking if we could hunt the area, he said, "Be my guests."

Right after breakfast we took Alex's dog Colonel, and my Silver Lady's Josephine, called Jo, then thirteen months old, across the road.

Shortly after we turned the dogs loose, Jo pointed near the edge of a swamp. I shot a woodcock when it flushed in front of her. She immediately went to retrieve, picked up the "Timber Doodle," came about twenty feet toward me, laid the bird down, and gagged a little. She then refused to have anything more to do with it.

The pheasant season also was open at this time around Saginaw, Michigan, where we lived, and Jo had pointed and retrieved many cock pheasants before going on this grouse hunting trip. However, after the woodcock episode near Lincoln, she refused to pick up any game birds until one day when she was seven years old.

Upon returning from a grouse hunting trip in late October 1942, I found a friend, Chuck Eckhart, sitting on our front porch. He was waiting for me because I had promised to take him pheasant hunting.

After unloading some of my gear and dogs, we took Jo down to the Little Prairie Farm south of Saginaw, Michigan, only a couple of miles west of our home.

On our way to the place we wanted to hunt, we stopped at Mr. Otto's house to ask permission. Mrs. Otto informed us that Mr. Otto was husking corn in the field at the north side of the area we wanted to hunt. I hailed Mr. Otto as we approached the area and he told us to hunt anywhere except the two ten-acre buckwheat strips.

Chuck and I turned Jo down on the west side of the area, where volunteer barley had come up after the harvest. Jo pointed well out in front and to our right, and we each bagged a nice cock pheasant when the birds took to the air.

We then swung around to our left, hunting to the west end of the field where there was a dike about ten feet higher than the field. A ditch, knee-deep with water and about thirty feet wide, ran along the near side of the dike.

When we approached the end of the field, Jo swam the ditch, went up on the side of the dike, which was covered with high weeds, and pointed. Not wanting to wade the ditch, I threw a clod of dry clay in front of the pointing dog. A huge cock pheasant rose, flying straight down the dike for twenty yards. Then it started across the ditch to our side and I shot. The bird fell right in the middle of the ditch, just floating. As Jo followed the flight of the bird, she came all the way across the ditch to where Chuck and I stood trying to figure out how we were going to get that bird without wading through the water, for I felt sure Jo would not retrieve it. "Chuck, let's go to my car. I'll get a check cord and tie a stick on one end, so when we come back I can throw the stick attached to the check cord over that rooster and gradually float it to shore on our side," I suggested.

While walking to the car Jo was alongside for a short distance, then left. I said, "We better watch Jo, she could point another pheasant." Hearing a splashing in the water and looking back we saw Jo in the ditch dunking the pheasant to get a grip on it. Finally she got a good hold on the bird, swam to shore, and brought the bird directly to me. From that day until she died, Jo retrieved every game bird that was shot over here—except woodcock.

Female woodcock. Spring 1979.

The Shock Collar As a Training Aid

The training collar or shock collar is an instrument to be used for a definite purpose. The manufacturers of this instrument have in mind not only bird dogs but also all other breeds of dogs. For example, it is used to stop yard dogs from chasing cars and to eliminate other foolish habits. However, when referring to the training of a bird dog, the dog must know absolutely what he is expected to do when a certain term is used. He must be taught positively to sit, heel, come, or whoa before a shock collar can be used on him for disobeying a command. The collar is excellent for breaking bird dogs from chasing undesirable game, such as deer, rabbits, squirrels, chipmunks, and so forth. Most unwanted game problems with grouse dogs crop up while working in the woods. The fact that these problems occur in the dense woods frequently makes it impossible actually to know that the dog is involved with a deer or other undesirable game. If you have the dog wear a bell in conjunction with the shock collar, you usually can tell by the sound of the bell if the dog is chasing something. For example, when the dog is bird hunting, the bell sound, "ding-a-de-ding-a-de-ding," is a definite pattern. If all of a sudden, the bell sounds "ding-a-de-ding" in a rapid-fire manner, the dog is chasing something whether you see him or not. Have the transmitter ready at all times, for this is most important when the dog's bell is ringing in a rapid-fire manner. *Do not blow your whistle. Do not call or yell at the dog.* Just shock him, then listen for the bell sound after the dog squeal has ceased. If the bell sound is in rapid-fire sequence again, shock him again, but still do not whistle or call the dog. Just listen for the bell. It is rarely that the dog needs a third shocking, since he usually will work his way back toward you with the bell denoting a hunting pattern.

The strategy of this training is that the dog thinks the deer or other game he was chasing is what shocked him. In other words, let the undesirable game break the dog from the habit. In the event that the dog is chasing a grouse or a woodcock, providing he is pointing birds staunchly the shock will not be harmful, because he should not be *chasing* birds.

There are certain breeds of bird dogs that have a natural running pattern. If it is natural for the dog to run extremely wide, it is unlikely that a shock collar will change or cure what comes naturally for that particular dog. There are dogs of various pointing breeds that have a natural way of keeping in touch with their handler/trainer while hunting without causing much concern. Once this type of dog is trained not to chase undesirable game, he will revert quickly to his natural hunting pattern and become a well-mannered grouse dog, all else being equal, such as being staunch on point, steady to wing (at least until the shot), then retrieving. It is better, of course, if he is steady to shot and also retrieves on command.

This brings up the subject of how to break bird dogs from chasing all birds.

One important thing to remember is: *never shock a dog with a bird on the ground.* Follow these simple directions: Take about six pigeons in a burlap bag to an open field or birdless area. Put the shock collar on the dog. I do not let the dog even see the transmitter. I carry it in my hip pocket. I am a firm believer in never letting the dog know I have anything to do with shocking him.

Turn the dog loose to hunt. When he comes reasonably near and you are sure he will see the bird, release one pigeon. Let the dog start chasing the pigeon. *Do not say anything,* just shock him. He will stop and most likely squeal a little. If he looks up at the pigeon while it is circling around and starts to give chase again, shock him, but say nothing. After the first pigeon has left the area I let the dog resume his running and hunting. I release a second pigeon where I am sure he will see it, and shock him the instant he starts to chase.

In my experience with the shock collar over the past five years, I have never had a dog chase the third pigeon released. The dog would stop to flush the instant he saw the flying bird.

It is important that you do not blow a whistle, say anything to the dog, or let him see you holding the transmitter in your hand (keep it accessible, but out of sight). The reasoning behind this system is that the dog thinks or feels that the flying pigeon or bird is causing the shocking sensation.

Remember, do not work the dog on any bird on the ground that same day before or after the treatment and do not work him at all the following day. The third day take him to the field again, with the training collar attached and a few pigeons in a bag. I would be willing to bet my old hat that your dog will stop to flush on the very first pigeon you release in his sight.

I have used this system successfully for the past five years with a Tri-Tronic Training Collar. (Thanks to Paul Long, an excellent bird dog trainer from Maiden, North Carolina.)

Please remember, do not use shock treatment on a puppy or young dog that is not already pointing controlled, liberated, planted, or wild native game birds.

In heavy cover the Beeper Collar is worn in addition to the bell and is a further aid in keeping track of a hunting dog. When the bell stops, the beeper is still audible, and the handler can therefore locate the dog more easily.

The Tattletale Beeper Collar for Cover Dogs

The Tattletale Beeper Collar for Cover Dogs is another product from Tri-Tronics, Inc. It is designed to be used on cover dogs either in conjunction with a dog bell or without a dog bell. A small horn-type speaker is mounted on the outside of the collar and slants away from the dog's ears so that the blasts from the beep tone do not hurt him. The beep tone sounds every four seconds, whether the dog is in motion or standing on point. The collar can be obtained in two different tones (high or low) so that two dogs can be worked together, each wearing a different-toned beeper.

Tobacco River Crockett wearing a Tattletale Beeper Collar while hunting.

The Dog Knows Best

A few years ago, I was grouse hunting in the late afternoon with two Setter dogs, Jim and Little Windy, south of Deerfield Center, Michigan. As I came out of the heavy woods to the high road which had steep banks on either side, I looked to my left and there stood both dogs, high and tight. With Jim backing, Windy was pointing towards a huge bog of six-foot-high shrubs. Since there was no way to get a shot, I threw a foot-long piece of wood down the steep bank ahead of the dog. A huge adult grouse flew out and straight over the scraggy shrubs. About halfway across, the No. 8 shot from my 20 gauge caused the grouse to dive into the bog, leaving many feathers drifting lightly above the shrubs.

Both dogs went into the boggy "shin-tangle" with me to hunt "dead," for they were both very good at finding dead birds and retrieving. Finding the spot where the grouse feathers were, Jim became very busy hunting close for the dead bird, but Windy kept going far out even though he was called back to hunt close several times. Since it was starting to get dark and Jim had not found the grouse, he was heeled up. Windy was left behind as Jim and I fought our way through the "shin-tangle" back to the road. Just as we neared the edge of the bog, I looked to see if Windy was coming. There he was—right behind Jim with that beautiful grouse in his mouth. The grouse was very much alive, for that long shot had only broken the bird's wing.

Believe your dog; he usually knows best. Bird dogs that hunt dead and retrieve are conservationists.

How to Make a Dog Release a Firm Grip on a Dead Bird

Some bird dogs hold onto a dead bird firmly. They seem to set their jaws. Even after fetching the bird they will not give it up. There is one sure method to get the dog to release the dead bird, and it doesn't matter whether the dog is standing or sitting after he fetches the bird. Place your left hand under his lower jaw towards the front so that you can take the dead bird when he does release it. Simultaneously, take hold of the dog's front paw with your right hand and squeeze gradually until the dog gives up the dead bird. At the same time that you squeeze the paw, say only the word "Give." After a few lessons, most dogs, when you reach down to them and say "Give," will be eager to please. A little praise after each lesson helps.

Your Dog's Sign Language

Learn all you can about the "sign language" your dog "speaks" with his tail. It tells you how your dog feels—happy, frightened, or cowed. (Some dogs are born timid. They usually don't make the best bird dogs.) As an example, there is the dog who carries his tail between his legs. This could be due to a fight with another dog, or because he was struck in the face or head as a reprimand. The latter should never be done, and, when you do reprimand the dog, never cuss, yell, or scream at him. His tail will tell you how badly he feels about this.

Adopt the procedure of taking the young dog to the field for a workout. You might be taking him in a dog cage in a station wagon or pickup truck. When your dog has had his workout and you are returning to your vehicle, call your dog in to load him into the cage. Do not grab him by the scruff of the neck or the hide in the middle of the back and throw him headfirst into the cage, while at the same time calling loudly, "Get in there, you #@/# blankety-blank dog." Once again, he immediately tells you with his tail that he is very unhappy about this kind of treatment.

I have seen individuals treat dogs in this manner, and it makes me feel sad. If you continue to do this, your dog will be reluctant and even resentful of coming to your vehicle. When he does come eventually, he will no doubt do so in a crawling motion with his tail down or under him. Avoid this kind of treatment. You can handle your young dog in an easy and pleasant manner, and you will then have a happy companion.

When you first take your dog to the field or woods for a workout, it is wise to call him in while you are some distance from your vehicle, snap the lead on him and lead him to your vehicle. When you arrive there, take the dog gently by the collar and raise his front end up towards the dog cage; with your right hand reach under his back end and give him a little boost, at the same time saying "Kennel-up," "Get in," or "Jump in." Whichever term you choose, use it consistently. I like the term "Jump in"; it has a good sound, and, in just a few workouts, the dog will come running to you when called and jump in by himself when told, with a happy, cracking tail.

About five years ago a man called me on the phone asking if he and a good friend of his could come the next morning to see our kennel, as well as our training grounds, and visit with me. At that time, one of the men was an executive vice-president of one of the big automotive firms; the other man was president of a plywood organization.

They showed up the next morning, a Saturday, at seven o'clock sharp. After the introductions, we all went to the kennel. There was a guard fence around the kennel in case a dog might get out of his run. After they looked at the kennel, I took the two men around the grounds so that they could see what type of cover and objectives there were where the dogs would be worked. When we returned to the house, the two gentlemen went to their car and brought out two Setters—good-sized, one-year-old pups named Baggs and Deke, litter brothers. "We're going to leave our dogs in your care, but can we come up and see them once in a while?" the men asked. I assured them they could.

Two weeks later, on a Friday evening, the auto executive called, asking if he and his friend could come up and see their dogs the next morning.

They showed up in field clothes at seven o'clock, and the three of us went to the kennel. They asked if they could let their dogs out in the play yard. I told them, "Of course." I was called to the phone, and, when I got back to the kennel, these two very prestigious men were on the grass playing with Baggs and Deke. The dogs were just as happy to see their owners. It never affected them during their training to have their owners come and see them.

I thought to myself when I saw these two men on the grass playing with their dogs, "These dogs will be companions for sure." They turned out to be good hunters as well, with stylish happy tails. Both of the men write to me periodically, and Tom always ends his letter saying, "Baggs is still my best friend," and Bill says the same thing about his dog. Baggs and Deke are two happy dogs. As a professional trainer, I got a lot of pleasure from seeing such a relationship between a man and his dog.

If you do have a young, eager dog that is reluctant to quit hunting and just keeps staying away a short distance running around and not coming when called, even though he knows what "come" means, do not get angry at him. Get him when you can, and, the next time you take him out for a workout, take him where there is no traffic so that you will have at least a couple of miles where you can travel by car. When you have worked your dog and are getting close to your vehicle, call him in. If he just runs around as before, get in your vehicle and start driving off slowly, watching the dog at the same time. He will start running alongside and might even try to race with you. Soon he will start slowing down, and, when he does, stop your vehicle. Get out and call the dog in. If he just stands off a short ways, get back in the vehicle and proceed slowly, and the next time you stop he will more than likely come running to jump in the cage. The dog finally realizes that you are trying to leave him, and he decides it is much nicer to ride. So dogs do think.

This type of dog is usually an enthusiastic hunter. Patience with him will prove very rewarding later on. I cannot stress too strongly how important it is to keep your dog happy while you are working with him.

Some people seem to think a dog does not have feelings, that he is just a dumb animal. They could not be more wrong. Dogs do have feelings, because if they did not, there would be no way in the world they could be trained by man.

Through the "sign language" of his tail, your dog shows his intelligence as well as his happiness. If he runs with a merry tail, he is happy—really hunting and happy about it.

A running dog may carry his tail in various styles and there are many different opinions as to what these styles mean. There is the high "dead" tail that moves only when the dog's hind feet hit the ground and then that tail will bob back and forth just a little. Then there is the high tail that has a rhythmical motion back and forth towards the head and back again. (Also, a dog that runs with his head high is considered to have good running style.) In another style the tail is held about half-mast; that is, halfway between straight up and straight out, with an up-and-down, side-to-side manner, in a rather circular motion. This shows an extremely happy hunting dog. As long as the dog points with his tail not lower than a one-o'clock-high position, it is also considered good style.

I have had seven Setters and a Pointer that hunted and pointed with the "half-mast" style, which I refer to as "a merry tail on a very happy hunting dog." All of these dogs proved to be excellent bird finders, and all of them handled every species of upland game birds well: pheasants, sharptail grouse, Hungarian partridge in South Dakota, bobwhite quail in the Southern states, and, of course, all of our upland game birds in Michigan, our home state. Four of these dogs also competed in field trials during the off-season. They gave good accounts of themselves in the trials, as well as being good stylish hunting dogs, proving to be pleasurable dogs in either area.

I am a firm believer in registering my dogs so as to keep a good record of the breeding programs. Listed here are six of the dogs which I have mentioned earlier in the book: Jurex's Silver Lady, whelped December 20, 1933, FDSB #230221; Silver Lady's Josephine, whelped July 21, 1935, FDSB #258466; Direct Heir's Dawn, whelped July 12, 1937, FDSB #277852; Windy's Pride, whelped June 24, 1937, FDSB #344756 and AKC #A554195; King's Chief General, whelped July 24, 1946, FDSB 397804; and Tobacco River Bill, whelped May 8, 1961, FDSB #663634—all English Setters. Pamela, a Pointer female that proved to be an extra-good, young grouse and woodcock dog with fine running and pointing style, met with an untimely accident at the age of fourteen months when a veterinary hospital where she was being kept caught fire and all the animals there perished.

Of these seven dogs mentioned, all with similar style, attitude, and strong desire to find and handle birds, Tobacco River Bill, a half-brother to Grouse Champion Ghost Train, was the outstanding dog. Bill was built like the "old timey" Setters, but he had the modern Setter style. He was considered a big dog—white, orange, with a few ticks of orange, weighing fifty-eight pounds in working condition. His size made up for his ghostly, quiet way of running in the grouse woods. Being ninety-eight percent white, he was easy to see. Bill was strong, intelligent, and willing to please, with an extremely good nose, and a determined desire to find and handle birds under all conditions. His willingness to be trained was astonishing. He was completely finished at seventeen months and staunch on point in or out of sight.

One time when Alton King was judging a trial in which Bill was competing, I overheard him say, "Tobacco River Bill is the best bird-handling dog I have ever seen." I learned more from the "sign language" of this dog's tail than any other dog I have worked over the years. Possibly, I felt a little closer to him than some of the other dogs to the extent that the dog seemed to understand how I operated, and I understood him. His tail spoke for him. He could be on a rigid point, both ends high, as I approached him to flush the bird. If the bird had run off, Bill would flick the end of his tail erratically and immediately break point (without a word from me) and run as fast as he could, stay on the downwind side of the running bird and swap ends into a hard stylish point. When Bill relocated, the bird was always there for me to flush. Bill himself never flushed a bird while relocating. His "talking" tail and superb nose worked well. Relocating on his own without orders is the difference between an intelligent dog and one that works only on command.

Dogs really do talk with their tails. What I have learned from their doing so has not only been pleasant and interesting but also sometimes amazingly educational. There is the pleasant, simple, everyday hello. You may just be walking by where your dog is lying in his doghouse or in a carrier in your vehicle. Even though he can't see you, he can recognize your footsteps or some other sign, and the tap, tap, tap of his tail lets you know he is there.

When you have a good shooting dog, the tail talk really pays off when you're hunting. Pay close attention when you turn the dog loose to hunt. If he runs with a merry tail, he is telling you that he is really hunting and happy about it to boot. As he runs along, he may slow down a little as he gets scent of game, then move up a bit and establish a rigid point. As you attempt to flush the bird in front of your dog and you do not get the bird into the air, watch your dog. If he is flagging the tip of his tail erratically, he is telling you the bird (or birds) is running. Do not whoa him or insist that he remain on point. Send him on. If he runs straight in on foot scent and routs the bird, correct him at once. A dog that works running birds well will move out to the side quickly and will stay almost always on the downwind side of the bird, thus giving himself the advantage when he positively relocates the bird. If he relocates in this manner, do not say anything to him. Talking to him only makes him over-cautious, and his points will not be positive much of the time. Let him do his relocating rapidly on his own. This develops confidence and what is known as good bird sense in your dog. Remember, if you have purchased good hunting stock, the chances are that your dog knows more about hunting birds than you do.

Other important tail talk is evident even in a six-week-old bird dog puppy. If it comes running to you with a merry tail, it feels good, happy, and alert. When a puppy has a dead, droopy tail and listless attitude, it is not feeling well and something should be done for it at once. The problem could be internal parasites, such as roundworms, hookworms, heartworms, tapeworms, or whipworms. Once the pup receives the proper medical attention, it should come back fast. Watch his tail; you can tell.

A happy dog is a pleasure. Do not destroy that. Learn to understand your dog's tail talk, and he will understand your method.

Tobacco River Crockett, July 1979.

Close-up of roading harness with drag chains, fitted on Setter bird dog. Photo by Wally Brzenk.

Trainer getting his early morning exercise with the dog in a roading harness. Photo by Wally Brzenk.

Mackjackie in a roading harness equipped with drag chains. Excellent for keeping a dog in condition. Photo by Wally Brzenk.

Creating a Desire to Retrieve

In 1949 I had a Setter dog named General King's Blackhawk, call name Smokey. By the age of three, he had become an excellent grouse dog, but there was one exception to this in that he did not retrieve. Smokey would go to a downed bird, and, if the bird was crippled, Smokey would stand with one foot on it but would not pick up the bird. Wesley Habermehl, a friend from Alpena, Michigan, told me that if Smokey would retrieve, he would buy him. The dog did not have the temperament needed to be force broken to retrieve, and Smokey had been an easy dog to break. Everything he did well, he did for praise. That was all the reward he seemed to require. A friend who hunted with me that fall and I had killed forty-four grouse over Smokey. The dog went to every dead bird, but he would not pick one up.

On another beautiful fall day I decided to go alone with Smokey to a favorite spot along the Chippewa River, a private area where I was allowed to hunt a few times each season. We arrived at the area about 3:30 in the afternoon. I had let Smokey ride in the seat of my pickup that day, instead of in the carrier in back. He seemed to act as if this was something special, and, as it turned out, it was—for both of us. I let Smokey out of the truck, and he sat there waiting for me to don my light hunting coat and get my Model 12-20 gauge with cylinder bore tube. I tucked my empty shotgun under the bottom strand of a three-strand barbed wire fence. Smokey went under, and I thought that I should do the same. I got my posterior down—well almost down, when I heard a little ripping noise. That's right—I received a three-cornered tear in the seat of my newly-acquired hunting pants! When one is going grouse hunting, what's a little rip in the pants? I was sure that Smokey didn't care—he liked me just as well with a hole in my pants.

Once on the other side of the fence, my shotgun loaded with light 20's, No. 8 shot, Smokey and I worked our way towards the high right bank of the river. The popples and oaks were a bit sparse along this bank. Here and there were large white pine stumps. Most of them were cut off four to five feet above the ground, indicating that the beautiful white pine had been lumbered off when the snow was deep. Smokey had been working well in front and on either side of me, searching for Mr. Grouse. As we approached the high bank, I came up over a knoll and saw Smokey pointing towards a dogwood thicket. As I moved in ahead of the dog, two grouse bolted out of the dogwood, one going across the river, the other flying off to the right towards a new Austrian pine plantation. I downed that one. I told Smokey to go fetch, from habit I presume, because I knew that he would not fetch the bird. He did stand by the bird until I arrived, then went on hunting. I decided it was time for me to try what I hoped would be the answer to Smokey's retrieving problem. I picked up the large adult grouse, walked over to a large white pine stump nearby, rested my 20 gauge where it would be safe, and sat down by the stump, holding the grouse in my hands in front of me. In two or three minutes Smokey came looking for me. I did not let on that I knew he was there. I kept stroking the bird and saying over and over as I stroked it, "Pretty bird." After about five minutes of this, Smokey came closer and was prancing his front feet up and down frantically. The hunting coat I was wearing was one of those where you could load the dead bird from the outside or from the front on the inside. I stood up and, while Smokey was watching me excitedly, I pretended I was putting the bird in my coat from the front. Instead, I let it fall to the ground by the stump, and, at the same time, I reached for my gun and walked off hunting. Smokey went hunting, too, but in a couple of minutes I saw him swing wide to the left and go back to the rear, which was something he seldom did. It appeared that my little plan was working. In two or three minutes I heard Smokey directly behind me, and, as I looked down, sure enough, there he stood with a happy tail going and that beautiful grouse in his mouth, as nicely as one could hope for. I sat right down on the ground, and I made a big fuss over him. This is important, and it paid off that day. Smokey pointed two more grouse within a half-hour, and I was lucky from a shooting standpoint. Smokey was even luckier, for he retrieved both grouse to my hand in a happy manner, and that day he became a completely finished grouse dog. (Smokey could also retrieve from a pond or a lake.) Needless to say, Wes Habermehl bought Smokey. Later, at a grouse trial, Wes told me that the dog was the best retriever he had had in a long time.

An Amazing English Setter

This dog is mentioned on other pages, but his abilities as a grouse and woodcock dog were so diverse that he has earned a place in the hearts of everyone who ever shot a gun over him. His registered name was Windy's Pride. He was from a Laverack strain and was registered in both The American Kennel Club Stud Book and The American Field Stud Book, his numbers being AKC #A554195 and FDSB #344756, respectively.

Windy's original owner, August J. Neberle of Saginaw, Michigan, (affectionately known as "Neb"), has been a friend of mine since college days. When Neb went overseas during World War II, Windy became mine. The night Neb brought the dog over, he said, "Even though Windy is a well-finished grouse dog, he is hard-headed." Windy was then five years old. He proved to be an amazing grouse dog until his thirteenth year and his last grouse.

After working Windy a few times, I discovered by some of his actions that he was deaf—not hard-headed. Many people hunted with Windy and me, and I am sure that they never detected his deafness through his actions.

One fall, the late Edward B. Flack and Charlie Burroughs, from Saginaw, Michigan, came up to hunt grouse with me over a weekend. I had told Ed about some of the outstanding things that Windy would do while hunting. Ed said, "Now Jack, you're pulling my leg." During the next forty minutes, Ed would see Windy accomplish three of his feats.

It was mid-afternoon on Saturday. While hunting on an oak ridge that ran alongside a very dense evergreen swamp, Windy pointed on the ridge. When the grouse flushed, it flew high over the tall swamp evergreens. After my 20 gauge spoke, the grouse sailed farther along before falling into the swamp. Charlie, who was down the side of the ridge near the swamp, said, "I know where that bird came down. I'll go in the swamp and find it." I told him that he did not need to go, for Windy would find it. Charlie did not believe me and ventured into that dense swamp looking for the dead or crippled bird. I tapped Windy on the head lightly, releasing him to go hunt dead and fetch. He was back in three minutes with the dead grouse.

Windy very seldom had an unproductive point. His nose was keen, his eyesight extremely sharp, and he always pointed staunchly, high-headed with a one-o'clock tail.

A short while later, Windy came up a steep slope on our right. As he topped the ridge in front of us, he whirled and pointed back toward the direction that he had come—a nice point, but no ground cover—only a large oak tree. As we walked down the side hill in front of the dog, a grouse flew out of the far side of the oak tree. Neither of us had a shot. Ed said, "That's two things you told me about Windy—best dead bird finder and that he would point grouse in trees. Well, I'll be."

By now we had hunted about half a mile to where the swamp narrowed. Ed and I crossed over to hunt the far side back towards our vehicle. After about ten minutes along this side of the swamp, we came to a huge log that just seemed to invite us to "sit a spell." Windy went on in and out along the edge of the swamp for a hundred yards or so. In about five minutes Windy came out of the swamp edge, faced us, wagged his tail merrily, then went right back in where he had come out of the swamp. Ed and I just sat, but I said, "Ed, I think Windy has a grouse located. I'll know in a couple of minutes." Sure enough, Windy came out at the same place that he had before, only this time he came right up to us, turned around wagging his tail, and started back again. "Let's go, Ed," I suggested. "Windy has a bird located."

We arose and followed the dog. He went in the narrow part of the swamp where he had gone in twice before,

Ruth Stuart with Windy's Pride and their five grouse, 1943.

crossed to the far side just short of three spruce trees that had branches nearly to the ground, and, at the very bottom of a steep slope on the far side, pointed beautifully and staunchly. We closed in. Windy had located not one grouse, but two. Ed stood with his gun on his arm as the two grouse exploded from under the spruces and flew straight up that steep side hill. I dropped to my knees to get a shot through the trees; the one bird had already topped the side hill, and the second one and the load from my 20 gauge apparently met at the top of the hill, because the grouse's tail fanned and turned straight up, then disappeared, I knew not where. "You missed," said Ed.

"Windy knows whether I missed or not," I replied.

With that, I tapped the dog on the head. He ran up that steep side hill, over the top, and was back in less than a minute with the very dead grouse.

We headed for the car. As we neared the road at the end of the swamp, Charlie came walking up.

"Where in the world have you been, Charlie?" Ed asked.

Charlie replied, "I've been looking for the grouse Jack shot that fell in that blamed swamp. I never did find it."

Another time Ed Flack went with me to West Branch, Michigan, for a weekend hunt with our Setters. Windy was a very proud dog, besides being somewhat of a showoff. We had a very good afternoon hunt around Lost Creek and Germaine's Mill. Our headquarters while there was the Ogemaw Hills Hotel. In the evening when we arrived at the hotel, after caring for our dogs, Windy was allowed to carry a grouse to the hotel because he could stay in the room with me at night. The hotel lobby was not large, but there were usually several people sitting around in chairs. Windy would carry his grouse around the lobby and out into the bar, showing everybody his bird. Some of the people, even Ed Flack, tried to get him to give them the bird. None of them knew the magic word. After showing off his bird, he would come to me where I sat on the steps of the open staircase and stand in front of me. I would whisper in his ear while holding my hand under his muzzle. I knew that he couldn't hear me, but nobody else knew that. Windy would lay the bird gently in my hand, come to heel, and we would go upstairs to our room.

Another weekend, I was with some friends from Traverse City at their cottage, Gobbler's Knob, on Bellew Lake, for grouse and woodcock hunting. Late Sunday, while hunting, Windy pointed a woodcock between the dirt road and the lake. After the shot, Windy came in to heel with the bird and carried it all the way alongside me to the cottage where our hosts had several guests. When we came to the door, my wife let us in. Windy went around the room showing everyone his bird. My, but he was proud!

Windy was bred into our Llwellyn Setters, which has indeed helped our class grouse dogs during the past forty years. Even today our six class Setters all trace back to Windy's Pride.

The fall that Windy was thirteen years old, I did not hunt him as much or as long as in previous years, but every time the dogs would be loaded to go, he would come out of his indoor kennel and beg to go along.

Coming in at about 4:45 one afternoon at the end of the season, I put the dogs from my pickup into the kennel. Windy came out begging to go one more time. I let him out of his kennel run, and he went straight to my truck. I helped him into the cab and onto the seat—he was happy. I stopped at the house to tell my wife, Ruth, that I was taking Windy to Greer's place for a little hunt. It was the last day of the season, and I wanted Windy to help me in the Grand Finale. It was only a half-mile to Greer's woods. As soon as we arrived, Windy was more than ready to go. After we got out of the truck, I loaded my trusty Model 12 Winchester with a couple of light loads of No. 8 shot. Cradling the piece in the crook of my left arm, I tapped Windy on the head and he was off. He made four or five quite brisk casts—not extensive but adequate—in a happy manner. We had gone only about two hundred yards, and, as I topped a knoll in the popples, there Windy stood beautifully, but his tail was at about two o'clock. He was pointing into a witch hazel thicket.

It was dusk, and I was walking quietly and carefully past Windy when two grouse erupted from under the witch hazel. One went straight away through the gray popples; the other flew high, giving me a little sky through the leafless trees for a background. I chose this bird. When my 20 gauge sounded, flame shone brightly at the end of the barrel. Feathers drifted lazily in the soft breeze as the grouse turned a somersault before falling dead to the earth. This time Windy did not wait for me to tap him on the head. He ran as fast as his legs could go, picked up the grouse, and came back and walked beside me to the truck with his bird. I helped him into the cab and up on the seat, and he sat straight up proudly with the grouse in his mouth all the way home.

When we arrived near the back of the house, I let Windy out of the pickup. He went straight to the back door. My wife, Ruth, let Windy in. He sat in front of her in the kitchen proudly holding his last grouse. "Whisper in his ear, Mama, and he'll give you the bird," I told her. She did so, and Windy placed the grouse carefully in her hand.

Windy left for the happy hunting ground the next summer, on July 27, 1950. A nice white-pine box was built for his last rest. I buried him on a grousy-looking knoll at the back of our kennel overlooking the Tobacco River.

False Pointing

Sometimes false pointing in a dog is man-made by playing too long at a time and too often with a feather on a fishing-pole line. This sort of exercise is good when puppies are six to eight weeks old. As soon as you find out the puppy shows a natural pointing instinct, this practice should be discontinued because it could get the dog into a false-pointing habit. Some older dogs can develop a false-pointing habit for various reasons. For example—constantly hiding birds under a windfall. If planted birds are needed to work your dog, be sure to hide the bird in a place where a wild bird would choose to hide—grassy or weedy fence rows, or open hay fields along the edges of wood lots. You can also hide the bird in the woods in a briar thicket, in an old stump where brush may be around it, and, once in a while, in a windfall, because birds, grouse especially, do use windfalls quite frequently. By using the above system, the dog learns to search all of the birdy places, not just a select few.

If your dog develops a false-pointing habit from your working him in the same area too often, especially if birds are hidden or released each time you work him, start taking the dog to a different area where there are no birds.

A dog can be discouraged from false pointing once you know he is obviously getting carried away with this practice. If you are sure, do not attempt to go flush a bird. Just walk on as though you don't see what he is doing—ignore him. Eventually he will come hunting with you. By all means, do not say anything to the dog; rather, completely ignore him. The handler must keep up his end of this treatment. However, if after several workouts like the above the dog still insists on false pointing, there is another treatment which almost always produces a cure. Once you have tried to flush a bird in front of the dog without results and you are sure he has false pointed, go to the dog, open his mouth and squirt a small amount of Bitter Apple in his mouth. Grannick's Bitter Apple is manufactured by Valhar Chemical Corporation and can be purchased from companies that handle dog accessories and supplies. Chewing tobacco is not my dish, but expectorating tobacco juice in the dog's mouth when he false points is the oldest of remedies.

The All-Day Hunter or Competition Dog

The difference between a top-flight, stylish gun dog and a grouse trial dog is the conditioning.

An ardent grouse hunter hunts his dog as long as it is able to run. Many people describe their dog as being an all-day hunter. This dog has to pace himself for the duration of the hunt.

One who wishes to enter his finished, top-flight, stylish gun dog in competition with other dogs in grouse trials should condition the dog gradually, starting with half-hour heats where the dog puts all of his effort forth the whole time. Each day, the time is increased for whatever type of grouse trial the dog is being conditioned, whether it be a one-hour or longer heat in a grouse classic or grouse championship.

The dog must be gotten ready for competition in such a manner that the dog will maintain his style and speed, handle his birds in a mannerly fashion, and put his best foot forward for the entire time of the ground heat or stake in which he is competing.

All one needs is a well-bred, classy dog with finished manners on bird handling. The owner-handler can go whichever way he chooses—all-day hunter, grouse-trial competition, or both. It is strictly a matter of conditioning.

"Unproductives"

"Unproductive" is a much better term than "false pointing," because failure to produce a bird may not be false pointing for various reasons. I have seen some of the top quail dogs have four to six unproductives in an hour's hunt on certain days. Maybe the late Henry P. Davis came as close to the answer as anyone when he wrote a feature article in *Sports Afield* a few years ago, entitled "Mother Earth Breathes."

A true grouse dog, regardless of breed, is altogether a different type of bird dog, mainly because the bird he hunts has a style of its own, and the type of terrain it frequents is also different: woodland with various deciduous trees on the flatlands and highlands, such as aspen, beechnut, white and red oak among various scattered pines; many shrubs, such as red and gray dogwood, hawthorne, Juneberry, witch hazel, wild raisin, blackberry briars, and bracken; and huge evergreen swamps throughout the rolling hills, flatlands, swamp edges, and potholes. That is the ruffed grouse's Michigan habitat, and he knows the avenues of escape in order to survive better than the hunter and his bird dog. A well-trained, finished grouse dog, one that is staunch on point (in or out of sight), can stop to flush, and is steady to wing and shot, is more likely to have an unproductive than one that is not completely finished. For example, in the fall of 1980, Wally Brzenk and I were working two finished Setters, call names Joe and Shiloh, on a private area that had just about all the cover and terrain mentioned earlier. Working along an old tote road on the low side of the area, both dogs had hunted the pine plantation and lowlands well, without birds. "Let's work the dogs through the beechnuts in the hills back of the cabin," Wally suggested. I agreed, since the grouse were not in the lowland. As we were walking up, nearing the top of a knoll, a grouse lifted about fifty feet ahead of us.

Turning to Wally, I said, "Did you see that grouse take wing?"

"I sure did," he answered.

"Let's stand here," I said. "We can learn what causes some of the unproductives. Shiloh is down in the pothole on your left; Joe is coming across fast from the right."

When Joe neared the spot from which the grouse had risen just ten seconds before, he stood solidly, high and mighty, for about twenty seconds, flagged his tail, broke point, and went on hunting. If this had happened in a grouse trial where the handler, as well as the judges, had not seen the grouse leave, the handler, seeing the dog stop, on point, might even have said "Whoa" to the dog, and then gone in front to flush the bird. The result would have been a big fat unproductive.

Another situation that can be an unproductive in the grouse woods is one in which you find your dog pointing a few feet from a clearing in the woods. More than likely the dog had a "stop-to-flush," even though you did not see or hear a grouse. There have been times when hunting crosswise over ridges and small valleys that, when topping a ridge, the dog could be seen pointing on the next ridge a few yards ahead. When the handler tries to flush but doesn't produce a bird, a young, green, broken dog may stay on point, especially if the handler says "Whoa"; however, after the broken dog has hunted grouse for a couple of years, he will learn to correct on his own. The term that applies here is "bird sense." As the hunter approaches the dog, he will flag his tail, break point, and do one of two things: If he had a "stop-to-flush" where the hunter did not see the bird, he will go on hunting, making complete casts; however, if, when he breaks point, he makes short, snappy, sometimes close circular casts, he will be trying to relocate a running grouse. This is not the time to start talking to him, saying, "Easy, careful now." Don't say anything to him. Let him get smart by himself, and you will have a whale of a good grouse dog with fewer unproductives. Know your dog.

A sensational style and type of point: a dog running with the wind behind him catches scent of the bird after he has gone by in full stride. A thrill to see.

1977 Lakes States Grouse Championship winners. Front, left to right: Thomas A. Novak with Ch. Jetrain, and Dave Hughes with runner-up Clizzeke B. Center: Rotating trophy. Rear, left to right: John Elford and Robert Baker, judges; Ken McLaughlin; Jack Stuart, Reporter. Photo by Jack Nicholson.

Litter brothers win 1978 National Amateur Grouse Classic. Left to right, Thomas A. Novak with Jetrain, runner-up, and Wallace J. Brzenk with Macjak, winner, with the Red Wing Trophy.

The Finished Pointing Bird Dog

A finished dog is one that may run in a one-course trial, where liberated or planted birds, usually quail, are used. The dog must be broken to stand the test of a bird (or birds) that just walks off in plain sight after he has established a point. Many times this happens when the handler goes in front of the pointing dog to flush the bird.

The dog also must be trained not to go directly to a marked bird after it has flown and set down at the end of its flight. He can be taught to go in the direction opposite from where the bird has flown, mainly because he will not get credit for a find on a marked bird. Besides, pen-raised birds generally do not fly well the second flight, and the dog could get involved in bad manners. It is wise to control the dog so as to encourage him to hunt for another bird.

A common pigeon is a very good bird to use when teaching a dog to stand solidly and watch a walking bird in the field where the handler regularly works the dog. Use two or three pigeons; I use three. The first pigeon is hidden and the second pigeon has both wings (flight feathers) cut back evenly with a pair of scissors. The amount cut back determines how high and how far the bird can fly.

Work the dog on the clipped-wing bird first. When the dog finds and points the bird, flush it. It will flutter, fly low for a short distance, and just walk around slowly. The dog must remain on point, let the handler shoot his blank pistol, and remain steady to shot.

When sending the dog on, take him by the collar, head him in the direction opposite the walking bird, and insist that he look for another bird. Work him in the area where you hid the first pigeon until he finds and points it. If the dog is a finished dog—that is, steady to wing and shot—the procedure here is routine. By having a third bird hidden, you can work the dog so that he can find it without going to the clipped-wing bird. This instills a willingness in the dog to hunt for birds other than marked ones.

Of course, the procedure above is done much more easily and in less time if one employs the Electronic Game Bird Releaser as shown.

This is important to dogs that run in grouse trials even though they run on contiguous courses; especially in the spring when grouse are not found easily.

The dogs that have run the best ground heats, though they might not have found and handled a grouse or woodcock, could be called by the judges to show on planted or liberated quail in a designated area. Only mature dogs and Derby-age dogs are subject to be, as the term goes, called back for a second series to prove themselves.

The author riding to Course 7 at the Gladwin Field Trial Area while reporting the National Amateur Grouse Championship in 1978. Photo by Vic Christopherson.

1979 Grouse Futurity, sponsored by the Grand National Grouse Championship, Inc. Winners: Front, left to right: Jim Tande with Heartbreaker, first; Wally Brzenk with Magic Man, second; H. Styles Bridges III, with Lightning Flash Birdie, third; Dale R. Hernden with Stargazer, fourth. Back row, left to right: Thomas A. Novak, Secretary; Richard Straub, judge; Jack Stuart, Reporter; Richard Brenneman, judge. Photo by Jack Nicholson.

1978 National Amateur Grouse Championship dinner at the King's Table, Prudenville, Michigan. Left to right: Basil S. Hawkins, judge; Vic Christopherson; Miss Leslie Anderson, AFTCA secretary, presenting a gift to Reporter Jack Stuart; Dale, Marti, and David Hernden. Photo by Wally Brzenk.

Alibi Hall at the grouse field headquarters, Gladwin Field Trial Area, Meredith, Michigan, where the trials are re-run during the Happy Hour. Alibis flow freely.

All the dog wagons, vans, dog trucks, and dog trailers gathered at Alibi Hall. The absence of people about indicates that they are in the Hall stuffing themselves with Mae Fruchey's family style dinners, at the 1981 Grand National Grouse Championship.

Turning two class Setters, Joe and Jackie, loose to hunt. Photo by Wally Brzenk.

Joe has the first find, and his half-sister Jackie honors him nicely. Photo by Wally Brzenk.

The Purpose of Field Trials

Field trials for pointing breeds of bird dogs have become increasingly popular over the years. Some of the more important events, the ground heats, such as the Open All-Age and the Championship Stakes, are of longer duration and they are run on native game birds.

There are also a great many field trial clubs now holding one-course trials, mainly because ample territory for consecutive courses is no longer available. These trials are generally run on liberated or planted birds, such as pheasants, pen-raised quail, and sometimes chukar partridge. Some of these clubs salt the whole course from one end to the other with liberated birds, while other clubs may have a designated bird field at or near the end of their regular course.

There are several good reasons why field trials have become so popular. Their main purpose, of course, is to improve the breed and the standards of all pointing dogs and to maintain these standards. By breeding top-notch field trial winners, male or female, hunting aptitude and style are maintained. In many cases, they are improved. Field trials are breeders' stakes with a purpose.

To prove a point, take a top-notch dairy farmer and breeder of extra-high-quality milk cows. This dairyman has five fine two-year-old heifers; four of these heifers give sixteen to twenty quarts of milk twice a day, but the fifth one is giving only four or five quarts twice a day. This one will never be bred again but will go for beef. This example is only to impress on the sportsman bird hunter how important pointing bird dog field trials really are.

Since this book places emphasis on grouse dogs and the training thereof, it is all-important that grouse dog field trials be given the space they so rightly deserve. The grouse trialers themselves are a closely knit fraternity. The social aspect of these groups is beyond reproach, yet the participants in the trials are competitive.

Top-flight grouse dogs are a breed apart from most other trial dogs; however, many good grouse dogs develop into fine shooting dogs on other game birds in many areas of the United States, Canada, Japan, and other countries.

A good, class grouse dog is what it is for various reasons. Class in a grouse dog consists of the following: running high-headed, with a smooth gait that allows him to stop the instant he scents a bird; pointing with head and tail high and, by all means, with a merry tail while running.

Now that class has been established, the dog must negotiate the dense woods quietly with speed, checking all the birdy places, of which there are many. At the same time, he should apply himself to the side and front of his handler, remembering, too, where his handler is going to be at a given time, so he can sight-check his handler without having to run right up to him.

A completely finished grouse dog capable of winning championships and shooting-dog stakes must be staunch on point (in or out of sight) and steady to wing and shot, must back his bracemate voluntarily if the opportunity presents itself, must stop to flush on an accidentally flushed or wild flushed bird if he sees the bird, and must handle kindly with a minimum of help either by voice or whistle from his handler.

There are a good many grouse hunters who own such a dog. They can really enjoy their dog for more than just the hunting season by joining a good grouse dog club and participating in the grouse trials.

There are grouse trial clubs in three or four states at present, and room for more. Two important ones in Pennsylvania are the Venango Grouse Dog Club and the Pennsylvania Field Trial Club. A new grouse trial club held two successful trials in Minnesota in the fall of 1980 and the spring of 1981. A welcome club, indeed. Much has been written throughout the years about the famous Gladwin Field Trial Area at Meredith, Michigan. There are four grouse clubs in Michigan making use of approximately 5,400 acres of state-owned grouse habitat, which has proven to be the best grouse trial grounds in America to date. No small game hunting is allowed in this area at any time.

Lake States Field Trial Club is one of the oldest clubs. Besides its complete spring trial each year, it sponsors the Lake States Grouse Championship each fall along with an Open Grouse Derby Stake.

Another fine club is the Beaverton Grouse Dog Club, in Beaverton, Michigan. It also utilizes the Gladwin Field Trial Area each spring with a complete Open Grouse Trial, plus an Amateur Shooting Dog Stake. In the fall there is the notable George Fruchey Memorial Grouse Dog Classic, The Wolverine Derby Classic, and an Open Puppy Stake. For the past few years, the Val-Pen Brittany Club has been sponsoring an open all-breed pointing dog grouse trial in spring and fall, besides its All Brittany Grouse Trials. The Ruffed Grouse Society (the Saginaw, Michigan chapter) was created and spearheade by two ardent grouse hunters and trialers, Dale R. Hernden and John A. Nicholson, both of Saginaw, Michigan. This club appeals to amateur trainer/handlers and their dogs, with but one exception. In the spring the club also sponsors the Ruth Stuart Memorial Open Puppy Stake.

This two-man club has successfully fought the odds caused by lack of club membership. The club started about 1976, sponsoring two amateur grouse classics in successive falls, then made a bid for an Amateur Grouse Championship. With the help of Miss Leslie Anderson (secretary of the Amateur Field Trial Clubs of America) and The American Field, the Amateur Grouse Championship was granted to this club. In conjunction with the Amateur Grouse Championship, the club runs The Jack Stuart Derby Classic. Up to this time there are amateur championships on all other game birds.

The top grouse championship club is the Grand National Grouse Championship, Inc. This is separate from all the other grouse clubs; however, many members from the other clubs are also members of the Grand National Grouse Championship Club. This championship is set up as a rotating club; i.e., it is run in one of three different grouse trial areas each year: New York State, Pennsylvania, or Michigan, but not necessarily in that order. However, when the bylaws and running rules were inaugurated, provisions were made that a committee be appointed each year to report to the president of the club about the grouse population in the area designated for the trial that particular year. If it is not sufficient to run a successful championship, the trial is run in the area where grouse are prevalent enough to assure a successful championship. This championship is the acme of all grouse championships. The Gladwin Field Trial Area in Michigan has had the honor of producing grouse champions every time other areas have relinquished their turn because of insufficient grouse population.

In order for a pointing bird dog to attain a grouse championship, he must run an intelligent, stylish ground heat, as well as point and handle a native grouse satisfactorily for the judiciary.

The Electronic Releaser is completely hidden in a weed patch with short grass on all sides before the dog is released to hunt the bird. The dog establishes a nice point, the bird is flushed, and the dog remains steady to wing. Photo by Wally Brzenk.

The birds lands right in front of the pointing dog and starts walking around as the dog remains steady. Photo by Wally Brzenk.

Macjak's first find in the 1977 National Grouse Invitational. By Kim McGuire.

Ch. Pleasant Valley Clyde. The wide collar is bright orange in order to help locate the pointing dog in dense cover.

Ch. Ghost Train.

GROUSE DOG CHAMPIONS

It is only natural that I go back many years about the number of good grouse dogs that have won championship titles on that glorious game bird, the ruffed grouse. The grouse dog that wins a championship on the modern-day grouse is indeed an artist in his hunting skill, with top-quality manners and style.

This constitutes a dog with good conformation, with style that indicates the dog is happy and is displaying a merry tail while hunting (the higher the better). He must be eager and willing to hunt the birdy places, and, at the same time, have contact with his handler as though he were on an invisible check cord. I mean that the dog responds to his handler by his own initiative, or to his handler's voice or whistle from greater distances, depending on the density of the cover. If he handles on his own initiative, it is more impressive.

His natural initiative created by his wisdom and past grouse-hunting experiences make it possible for him to hunt the right places for grouse and, when a grouse is found, to have the extreme bird sense to handle this king of all game birds properly and with style, to point intensely and staunchly, to allow his handler to flush the birds, and to stand solidly to the flight of the bird and the shot. For this latter quality, the term is "steady to wing and shot." The dog is not to move until released, or ordered by his handler to go on hunting. While he is in the act of hunting, if a grouse or woodcock flushes wild where he can see it, he must stop to flush, indicating his training and good manners. Also, he must, if the opportunity presents itself, honor or back his bracemate voluntarily. He must maintain his hunting application with vigor throughout the entire ground heat—which indicates superb stamina. All this must be done with a minimum of handling.

To qualify to run in a grouse championship, a dog must have placed first, second, or third in any of the following stakes in an Open Stake Trial: All-Age, Shooting Dog, or Derby.

To qualify for an amateur grouse championship, the dog must have placed first, second, or third in an Amateur All-Age, Amateur Shooting Dog, or Amateur Derby Stake, and must be handled by an amateur handler.

Also, to qualify, the trials, be they Open or Amateur, must be recognized trials that are advertised in *The American Field* magazine at a designated period prior to the actual running of such trial and run under minimum requirement rules, which are published in *The American Field* magazine.

I have judged both Open and Amateur trials over the years and have had conversations with people who do not understand the difference between Open and Amateur trials. The judging standards are the same for Open and Amateur trials. The only difference is the handlers. A professional bird dog trainer cannot run a dog in an Amateur trial, but an amateur handler can enter and handle a dog in both Open and Amateur trials. For example, until April 1981, I was classified as a professional trainer. My own dog, Tobacco River Crockett, was qualified to run in Open grouse championship trials, and I wished to get the dog qualified to run in the Amateur grouse championship trial. John A. (Jack) Nicholson, an amateur, placed my dog second in the Wolverine Walking Shooting Dog Stake in the fall of 1979, which qualified him for the Amateur Grouse Championship.

There are many grouse hunters who have a dog which they use to hunt grouse and woodcock and which meets the qualifications previously mentioned, except for a placement in a recognized trial. Take your dog to a grouse trial. Enjoy your good grouse dog the whole year, not just during the hunting season.

The following, besides being excellent grouse and woodcock gun dogs, have proven their excellence in grouse and woodcock trials, including championship stakes.

Ch. Pleasant Valley Clyde: Owned and handled by Dr. James E. Stiteler, DuBois, Pennsylvania. Clyde had thirty-four grouse trial wins, including six grouse championships and three placements as runner-up to champions, as follows: Lake States Grouse Champion, 1973-1976; Grand National Grouse Champion, 1976-1979; Pennsylvania Grouse Champion, 1976; National Amateur Grouse Champion, 1978; Grand National Grouse Champion Runner-up, 1975; Lake States Grouse Champion Runner-up, 1975, and Runner-up Champion in the Pennsylvania Grouse Championship, 1975; George Fruchey Grouse Dog Classic, 1976, and National Grouse Invitational, 1976. In a letter dated August 2, 1981, Dr. Stiteler wrote, "Clyde was truly a great dog and companion."

Ch. Ghost Train: White, orange, and ticked Setter; owned and handled by Wayne Fruchey, Beaverton, Michigan. Ghost Train, called Rusty, won the Grand National Grouse Championship in the fall of 1969 at the age of five. Not only did he have nineteen grouse trial wins, including his championship, but he also has been a great producer of winners since 1969, having, to date,

Ch. Macjak.

Ch. Ghost Star, 1978 Grand National Grouse Champion, by Ch. Ghost Train ex Hi Kaliber Tiny. Owner, Terry O. Shermoe, Lansing, Michigan. Handler, Bryant Shermoe.

The Class Train, with her proud owner Thomas Fruchey, from Beaverton, Michigan. Besides being Tom's private grouse hunting dog, the Class Train in 1980 won the National Amateur Grouse Championship, the Pennsylvania Grouse Championship, the Beaverton Grouse Dog Club Open Shooting Dog Stake, and was runner-up in the George Fruchey Grouse Classic.

Ch. Sam L's Meteor.

Ch. Jetrain.

Ch. Saturday Night Zeke.

fifty-five progeny that have accumulated a total of 280 wins. Most of the wins are grouse trial wins. Ch. Ghost Train has been a boon to grouse dogs in Michigan and elsewhere. Among his progeny are five that have become champions: Jetrain, a double champion; Ch. Macjak, a litter brother of Ch. Jetrain; Ch. Ghost Star; Ch. Sam L's Meteor; and Dales Deputy, winner of an Amateur Shooting Dog Championship in Japan.

Ch. Macjak: White, black and ticked Setter whelped July 25, 1972; owned, trained, and handled by Wallace (Wally) J. Brzenk of Detroit, Michigan. Mac won the North American Woodcock Championship in the fall of 1977. Besides the woodcock, Mac had two outstanding pieces of bird work on grouse during this championship trial at Moncton, New Brunswick, Canada. Mac maintained his prospects as an outstanding grouse dog from the very beginning when he placed third in the Grand National Grouse Puppy Classic in the spring of 1973 in a field of thirty-one puppies. To date, Mac, as a Ch. Ghost Train progeny, has compiled more wins than all other Ghost Train dogs: thirty-five wins—one Puppy, seven Derby, and twenty-seven Shooting Dog. Among these are the National Grouse Invitational, spring 1977, sponsored by the Lake States Field Trial Club and reported by the author for *American Field* magazine; and the National Amateur Grouse Classic, sponsored by the Ruffed Grouse Society (Saginaw, Michigan Chapter), spring 1978. Mac was sent to Japan on January 17, 1979. Before Mac left, I had the privilege of reporting his performances in many grouse trials, besides personally gunning over him for grouse and woodcock many times with Wally Brzenk.

Ch. Ghost Star: White-and-orange Setter bitch, by Ghost Train ex Hi Kaliber Tiny; owned by Terry O. Shermoe, Lansing, Michigan; call name Star. Both Terry and his son Bryant have hunted over Star, and many grouse and woodcock have been bagged over this stylish, young Setter. Then to put the icing on the cake, Star has accumulated about thirty grouse trial wins. Among them are the International Woodcock Championship in Fredericton, New Brunswick, Canada, 1977; The Grand National Grouse Championship, 1978; and the Lake States Grouse Championship, 1980. Bryant Shermoe handled Star in these titular events, as well as in the regularly sanctioned grouse trials.

The Class Train: Sired by Fascias' Nickey ex Myatt's Cricket. An outstanding Setter bitch, The Class Train has been developed by her proud owner, Thomas Fruchey, one of the youngest present-day amateur trainer/handlers in the Michigan grouse woods. Nan, as she is affectionately called by her owners, has been a consistent winner since 1978, her first year as an All-Age, placing first in The George Fruchey Grouse Shooting Dog Classic that year and again in the fall of 1979. The fall of 1980 was Nan's best season, for she won the National Amateur Grouse Championship, was runner-up in The George Fruchey Grouse Dog Classic, the winner of the Beaverton Grouse Dog Club's Open Shooting Dog Trial, and also winner of the Pennsylvania Grouse Championship. Quoting from a letter received from Thomas Fruchey: "Nan has never cost me a cent to run her in field trials because she won more prize monies than were spent in entry fees. Nan is still one of my best friends."

Sam L's Meteor: White, orange, and ticked Setter dog, sired by Ch. Ghost Train ex Hi Kaliber Tiny; owned by Sam R. Light, Punxsutawney, Pennsylvania; and trained by Richard Tuttle, Johnsonburg, Pennsylvania. Meteor's call name is Beau. He was an extremely hot competitor as a Puppy and a Derby. Beau's sparkle, style, and stamina are very obvious. As an All-Age dog, he has acquired twenty-three wins to date, including the Pennsylvania Grouse Championship in 1979. He won the Pennsylvania Grouse Dog of the Year award in the summer of 1980. He also has produced some winning progeny.

Ch. Jetrain: White, black, and ticked Setter dog, by Ghost Train ex Rockybelle; originally owned and trained by Thomas A. Novak, Hope, Michigan, but now owned by Burnt Creek Kennels in North Dakota. Jetrain won the Grand National Grouse Championship in 1975 and the Lake States Grouse Championship in 1977. Tom bagged many grouse and woodcock over Jet while he owned him. On top of this, Jetrain compiled twenty grouse trial wins and produced twenty dogs that have accumulated fifty wins to date.

Saturday Night Zeke: A very proficient Irish Setter, owned and trained by Reuel H. Pietz, Saint Cloud, Minnesota. Zeke to date has accumulated wins and is accountable for progeny with wins. I reported a grouse championship at the Gladwin Field Trial Area, in which Zeke was competing at the age of ten years. His ground race was exceedingly strong and stylish. Many grouse hunters will be interested in Mr. Pietz's thoughts on a grouse hunting dog. In a letter I received from him, he said, "Too many hunters have the mistaken impression that field trial dogs cannot be used for hunting. I've shot grouse and other game birds over Zeke since he was a pup."

The Pat Finder: Tri-colored Setter dog, by The Rock's Return ex Redwood Jill; owned by Jim Tande, Akeley, Minnesota. Pat was not extensively run in trials, but was hunted over very much in Minnesota after Jim and his family left Michigan; however, the Tandes came back to Michigan during the fall trials and ran Pat, and he won the Lake States Grouse Championship.

Elhew Flying Dutchman: White-and-liver Pointer, by Elhew Knickerbocker ex Elhew Patricia. "Dutch" captured the Grand National Grouse Championship in 1974. I reported this coveted event for *The American*

Ch. The Pat Finder. McKenna Studios.

Ch. Elhew Flying Dutchman.

Ch. Dale's Deputy.

Kumari Elhew Suzie, 1979 National Amateur Grouse Champion.

Field and recall one of the judges saying to handler Richard C. (Dick) Shear, as he was going in to flush the bird on Dutch's fourth grouse find in less than fifty minutes, "Why don't you put cotton in one of his nostrils?" This emphasizes the dog's keen nose and hunting ability. Dutch's conformation, style, and graceful stride exemplify the quality breeding program carried on by Robert G. Wehle at Elhew Kennels.

Ch. Dale's Deputy: White, orange, and ticked Setter dog, by Ch. Ghost Train ex Kipper; owned by Dale R. Hernden, Hemlock, Michigan. Deputy's dam ran out of milk when he was four and a half weeks old. Dale was notified by Wayne Fruchey of Ghost Train Kennels, so the pup was picked up at this early age and cared for by Dale—and even acquired his call name, Briar. Briar received his early hunting experience as a puppy on native quail near Jack, Alabama. He put his exceedingly good style and common sense to use in the Michigan grouse woods by being a top contender in grouse trials and doing some winning. He was sold and on November 21, 1978, was shipped to Japan where he won a regional Amateur Championship in the fall of 1979. Japan's gain was our loss.

Kumari Elhew Suzie: White-and-lemon Pointer bitch; the personal grouse shooting dog owned by amateur handler Victor J. Christopherson, Lansing, Michigan. Suzie, as she was affectionately called, provided many thrills for her owner as a grouse gun dog, besides being a top-flight, grouse trial competitor in winning many grouse Shooting Dog Trials. She improved her status as a fine, stylish, and mannerly grouse dog by winning runner-up honors in the inaugural running of the National Amateur Grouse Championship in 1978. In 1979 she rose to the very top by winning top honors in the second running of the National Amateur Grouse Championship prior to being shipped off to Japan.

Readers could find a note of encouragement in that, with the exception of Sam L's Meteor and Tobacco River Bill, all of the champion dogs included above were trained and handled by amateur bird dog owners.

Tobacco River Bill: White, orange, and ticked Setter dog, owned by Fred Renas, Gladwin, Michigan. Bill compiled twenty wins, all of which were grouse or shooting-dog wins, except one which was a first-place Open Derby in the Beaverton Grouse Dog Trial in May 1963. While Bill was a "hard luck" dog, he was always a contender to be reckoned with. His best win was when he ran in the first and only Ohio Grouse Dog Classic, southeast of McArthur, Ohio. Bill ran in the rugged mountain courses, having a voluntary back and a good find on grouse that were tucked away in a piney thicket high on the side of the mountain, which made him the classic winner. Tobacco River Bill, Kenru Sam, and Spartan Sage were litter brothers out of Samson Montcalm ex Mild Breeze. All three were winners as well as excellent gun dogs.

Tobacco River Crockett: White, orange, and ticked Setter dog, sired by Chief Cornstalk ex Crockett Maggie, owned and trained by Jack Stuart. His call name is Joe. He was an eye appealing individual, even as a young puppy. However, Joe did not receive very much exposure to training until he was more than two years old, due to illness in the family.

Once he got started, Joe trained easily and rapidly, because he possessed remarkable intelligence, a keen nose, willingness to accept training, and a desire to please. He developed into a delightful grouse and woodcock dog, as well as a pleasure to gun over, and a very close companion to his owner.

Joe has run in grouse and woodcock trials only sparingly, yet has won or placed several times. He topped off his trial accomplishments May 8, 1982, by winning the Ruffed Grouse Society (Saginaw Chapter) Amateur Grouse Classic.

Tobacco River Bill.

Tobacco River Crockett, winner of the 1982 Ruffed Groused Amateur Classic.

FIELD TRIAL CHAMPIONS

The two dogs pictured here and the one pictured at the top of page 110 are champions in their own right—on game birds other than grouse and woodcock, such as pheasants, chukars, quail, prairie chicken, and sharptail grouse (generally referred to as "chicken").

These dogs are usually hunted and handled from horseback in field trials and are considered gentlemen's high-class, horseback shooting dogs in the Deep South.

Ch. Shalimar and Ch. Red Water Jupiter with their trainer/handler, Dave Grubb.

Ch. Rhinestone Cowboy, honored by his son Memphis Cowboy. Photo by David Grubb.

Ch. Little John Boy. Photo by David Grubb.

A DERBY DOG

Rocky River Crockett: White, black, tan, and ticked Setter dog, sired by Tobacco River Crockett ex Deadwood Rubalou, owned by Terry DePuis, Blanchard, Michigan.

Rocky has proved to be an outstanding young Setter, having won or placed eight times in grouse and woodcock Derby and Shooting Dog Trials by the time he reached the age of twenty-two months.

He was Michigan Grouse Derby Dog of the Year while still a puppy. His latest achievement was placing second in the Grand National Grouse Futurity in November 1982, in a field of thirty-six entries.

Rocky River Crockett.

By P. G. Camstra.

These Denlinger books available in local stores, or write the publisher.

YOUR DOG BOOK SERIES

Illustrated with photographs and line drawings, including chapters on selecting a puppy, famous kennels and dogs, breed history and development, personality and character, training, feeding, grooming, kenneling, breeding, whelping, etc. 5½ x 8½.

YOUR AFGHAN HOUND
YOUR AIREDALE TERRIER
YOUR ALASKAN MALAMUTE
YOUR BASENJI
YOUR BEAGLE
YOUR BORZOI
YOUR BOXER
YOUR BULLDOG
YOUR BULL TERRIER
YOUR CAIRN TERRIER
YOUR CHIHUAHUA
YOUR DACHSHUND
YOUR ENGLISH SPRINGER SPANIEL
YOUR GERMAN SHEPHERD
YOUR GERMAN SHORTHAIRED POINTER
YOUR GREAT DANE

YOUR LHASA APSO
YOUR MALTESE
YOUR MINIATURE PINSCHER
YOUR NORWEGIAN ELKHOUND
YOUR OLD ENGLISH SHEEPDOG
YOUR PEKINGESE
YOUR POMERANIAN
YOUR POODLE
YOUR PUG
YOUR SAMOYED
YOUR SHIH TZU
YOUR SILKY TERRIER
YOUR ST. BERNARD
YOUR VIZSLA
YOUR WELSH CORGI
YOUR YORKSHIRE TERRIER

OTHER DOG BOOKS

A GUIDE TO JUNIOR SHOWMANSHIP
THE BOSTON TERRIER
BOUVIER DES FLANDRES
BREEDING BETTER COCKER SPANIELS
THE CARDIGAN HANDBOOK
THE CHESAPEAKE BAY RETRIEVER
CHINESE NAMES FOR ORIENTAL DOGS
THE CHINESE SHAR-PEI
DOGS IN PHILOSOPHY
DOGS IN SHAKESPEARE
DOGS ON THE FRONTIER
THE DYNAMICS OF CANINE GAIT
GAELIC NAMES FOR CELTIC DOGS
GERMAN NAMES FOR GERMAN DOGS
GERMAN SHORTHAIRED POINTER
GREAT DANES IN CANADA
GROOMING AND SHOWING TOY DOGS
THE IRISH TERRIER
THE KERRY BLUE TERRIER

THE LABRADOR RETRIEVER
LEADER DOGS FOR THE BLIND
THE MASTIFF
THE PHARAOH HOUND
MEISEN BREEDING MANUAL
MEISEN POODLE MANUAL
DOG OBEDIENCE TRAINING MANUAL VOL. 1
DOG OBEDIENCE TRAINING MANUAL VOL. 2
MR. LUCKY'S TRICK DOG TRAINING
RAPPID OBEDIENCE & WATCHDOG TRAINING
DOG TRAINING IS KID STUFF
DOG TRAINING IS KID STUFF COLORING BOOK
HOW TO TRAIN DOGS FOR POLICE WORK
SHOW DOGS—PREPARATION AND PRESENTATION
SKITCH (The Message of the Roses)
THE STANDARD BOOK OF DOG BREEDING
THE STANDARD BOOK OF DOG GROOMING
TOP PRODUCERS—SIBERIAN HUSKYS
YOU AND YOUR IRISH WOLFHOUND

To order any of these books, write to Denlinger's Publishers, P.O. Box 76, Fairfax, VA 22030

For information call (703) 631-1500   VISA and Master Charge orders accepted.

New titles are constantly in production, so please call us to inquire about breed books not listed here.